Savage Luxury

The Slaughter of the Baby Seals

BRIAN DAVIES

TAPLINGER PUBLISHING COMPANY
NEW YORK

First published in the United States in 1971 by
TAPLINGER PUBLISHING CO., INC. New York, N. Y.

Library of Congress Catalog Card Number 70-149046

International Standard Book Number 0-8008-6998-2

Manufactured in the United States of America

Contents

Illustrations

Dedication

So many have helped the seals. Some, like the Canadians who organized the nation-wide attack on the House of Commons, Fisheries and Forestry Committee, and like Alice Herrington, president of FRIENDS OF ANIMALS, only briefly mentioned in this story, have actually played major roles in the crusade for these lovely animals. Others, not even mentioned, have given much to the seals—and it is to these loyal friends and co-workers that I dedicate this book. People like:

U.S.A.
Keating & Virginia Coffey
Bill & Carol Brown
Adele Starbird
Mr. & Mrs. Francis L. Blewer
Mr. & Mrs. Alex. M. Lewyt
Regina Frankenberg
Mr. & Mrs. Kingsley Moore
Natalie Stevenson

CANADA
Officers & members of the Association for the Protection of Fur Bearing Animals

Officers & members of the Canadian Society for the Prevention of Cruelty to Animals

The British Columbia Society for the Prevention of Cruelty to Animals & many of its Branches

HOLLAND
Annelies Hoefer
Dick van den HOORN

SWITZERLAND
Max Jost
Jean Marchig
Mr. & Mrs. Schmidheiny
Claire Goel

Officers & members of the World Federation for the Protection of Animals

UNITED KINGDOM
Officers & members of Beauty Without Cruelty

Sidney Hicks
John Pitt

FRANCE
George & Joanna Bremond

AND TO ALL THE MANY OTHER FRIENDS OF THE SEALS

CHAPTER ONE

"An International Black Eye"

MR. McGRATH (*Committee Member*): ... Now, Mr. Chairman, I am really directing my remarks at you; if it is the intention of the committee to pursue this investigation into the seal fishery and the consequences of some of the films that have been produced and some of the activities of Mr. Brian Davies ... that we should now decide to call these people, and if you would entertain a motion, Mr. Chairman, I would move ...

MR. SMITH (*Committee Member*): As far as calling them is concerned, surely all we can do is invite them. We cannot ...

ANON. MEMBER: Get them in here!

THE CHAIRMAN (*Mr. Guy Crossman*): Order. Order.

ANON. MEMBER: ... by the scruff of the neck!

THE CHAIRMAN: Before we call the meeting we would have to be certain when the witnesses can be present.

MR. McGRATH: Mr. Davies is going to suggest to you that he can never come. He is being called by the Committee; he is being subpoenaed. He has to come when we want him.

THE CHAIRMAN: Is he in the Country, though?

MR. McGRATH: Bring him back; no matter where he is, bring him back.

THE CHAIRMAN: There is always the time factor in calling a meeting ...

MR. McGRATH: You can find him anywhere in the world. Bring him back.

It was Tuesday, March 18th, 1969, and the Canadian House of Commons, Standing Committee on Fisheries and Forestry, was considering the seal hunt and the fury it had aroused. Here is how the testimony[1] had started:

HONORABLE JACK DAVIS (*Minister of Fisheries*): ... I am tempted to say a word about seals before the questions start. Perhaps I could allude to the correspondence we have been getting in my office alone on the subject. We have already had one thousand two hundred and sixty letters in the English language and five hundred and eighty in the French language which we have answered. We have a backlog, I am told, that has really begun to pile up in the last few days, of about seven thousand, so we have a long way to go, but we are getting there.

This is probably the biggest volume of mail that anyone has been getting in Ottawa recently, but it is nothing when compared with some of the mail that our embassies have been getting overseas, as a result of *Paris-Match*.

MR. McGRATH (*Committee Member*): Is the Prime Minister's mail included in that figure?

MR. DAVIS: No, that is just my own.

MR. McGRATH: Do you have a figure on what the Prime Minister's mail has been?

MR. DAVIS: It runs into the thousands.

MR. McGRATH: I know that, yes.

MR. DAVIS: I am told that as a result of the several pages of colored reproductions in the European publication, *Paris-Match*, there has been a tremendous outburst of concern, particularly in France, Switzerland and Belgium. I am told our Embassy has had to deal not only with many thousands of protest calls and letters, but the Ambassador has had to defend our cause publicly against editorial criticism by the major Brussels news-

---

[1] Throughout this book the exact sequence of questions and answers at committee hearings is not followed, but the partial transcripts fairly represent, in my opinion, the tone of the particular meeting.

papers. The Embassy has received protesting delegations, one of which delivered a petition reportedly containing 400,000 signatures of school children and they have had to seek police protection against one bomb threat. In France a protest delegation marched into the chancery two or three weeks ago led by a man who has since gone on a much-publicized hunger strike. The group was later dispersed by the police. In Geneva our Consulate was similarly visited by student protesting groups, etc., etc. There was picketing in New York, Washington and so on, and our Embassy in Washington has been getting letters at the rate of 600 a day. Much of this activity has been caused by publications like the one in *Paris-Match* or by a several-page article which is appearing in the current edition of *Life Magazine*—and also, I think to an even greater extent by television. I was particularly concerned about a television program which was shown in New York City a few weeks ago—I will find the particulars as I will have to be careful about this—on February the 20th, in which Mr. Brian Davies who is Executive-Secretary of the New Brunswick Society for the Prevention of Cruelty to Animals was interviewed and in which he said in an answer to a question at the beginning of the television program that all of the young seals were skinned alive.[2]

We have the text to that interview and I think this Committee—certainly a committee of the House of Commons—should invite Mr. Brian Davies to come here and confront him with the transcript of that particular interview. It was part, as I said, of a television program in which the seal hunt was shown in color for a considerable period of time. As many of you know who have been to the hunt, it is a very gory happening and the film itself causes a good deal of consternation especially among women and children. If the expert who was interviewed and whose voice was heard along with the film made claims such as that which were untrue, it certainly hurts not only the seal hunt and, then, the fishery of

[2] I said no such thing. B.D.

eastern Canada, but I suggest even more important it hurts Canada's reputation.

I looked at the administration budget of the Department of External Affairs for this current year and it is about 50 million. I would think it would take quite a few million dollars to offset the adverse publicity which Mr. Brian Davies has given Canada as a result of his recent activities, not only in New York, but abroad.

MR. LUNDRIGAN (*Committee Member*): ... I am going to push the matter of the seal fishery because it is an issue that has to be clarified. We have on our hands an international problem, not merely a national problem or an east-coast Canadian problem.

The Minister was quite frank—and I am very happy that he was—in bringing out some of the incidents such as the one in New York and the other kind of publicity leading up to the international black eye, that we have received ...

... Can the Minister tell us whether his Department or the Government has taken any action, or plans any action, to have some of these matters refuted in such a way as to reshape public opinion, because, as has been admitted, we have suffered an international black eye.

This would not be so bad if we deserved it, but when it is realized that much of the publicity has been the result of fabrications and, as I understand it, fraudulent manufacturing of films and other such procedures to get attention—I will not give any examples. I want to be fair. As the result of this, has any action been taken or is any action contemplated?

What had caused this angry debate? What seals and where? Who had given Canada an "international black eye"?

Each year, in late winter and early spring, in the Gulf of St. Lawrence, that huge inland sea near the east coast of Canada, bounded on three sides by the mainland and denied easy access to mother North Atlantic by the granite block of island Newfoundland, hundreds of thousands of

12

harp seals and hundreds of hooded seals end their southern migration and congregate on the rafting ice pressing in on the shores of the Magdalen Islands, Prince Edward Island, and Newfoundland They turn the Gulf into a huge, natural nursery of incredible beauty, as the seal mothers give birth to their pups on the floating ice. Each mother bears one single pup. But, for generations, the hunters have gone after the seals because seal oil and pelts are in demand in the markets of the world.

Nineteen Sixty-Four was to be a turning point for these much abused animals. The unbelievable savagery and bloodiness of the hunt was filmed by a team of French-Canadians from *Artek Films* of Montreal. An outraged Europe and Canada demanded, first, improvements, and then, under the constant prodding of the New Brunswick Society for the Prevention of Cruelty to Animals "Save the Seals" Fund, and later the International Fund for Animal Welfare, Inc., with myself as spokesman, *outright abolition.*

Five years later, on Tuesday, March 18th, 1969, and Thursday, March 27th, 1969, the Canadian House of Commons, Standing Committee on Fisheries and Forestry, had heard from federal officials whose job it was to try to eliminate cruelty from the massacre, and to still the bitter domestic and foreign criticism of the now infamous seal hunt.

This book tells part of the agony, the triumphs and the setbacks of the men and women in their fight, to "expose" the hunt. Readers will see a pattern develop as we seek "coverage" in major publications. People need to know, before they can condemn.

CHAPTER TWO

The 1964 Hunt—Abolition versus Control

IN 1964 the hunt first achieved *widespread* public attention. It was carried on just as it had been for many years.

Hunters in aircraft surveyed the Gulf of St. Lawrence, and searched for ice conditions they knew would appeal to seals about to pup. When groups of seals were spotted, word went back to the mainland and hundreds of hunters descended on the animals by aircraft and ships. The females were killed or driven into the water as the slaughter commenced.

The baby harp seals, which comprised by far the bulk of the kill in 1964, are little balls of white fluff with huge dark eyes that cry great tears as hunters approach. Boasting of seven ways to kill seals, none of them designed for people with queasy stomachs, the killers went about their grim task.

Gaffing was the traditional method of the Newfoundland sealer. All he needed was a length of wood with a hook and a spike attached to one end. He struck the seal across the head with the hook or drove the spike into its brain. This method was used mostly on babies because they could not escape. Unfortunately, the spike sometimes missed a vital spot and only injured the seal.

Clubbing was another way. The hunters used wooden clubs like baseball bats, or great iron hooks. This was not

14

always satisfactory either, because baby seals often pull in their heads when alarmed. Their skulls become covered with a thick layer of fat, and it is anybody's guess how many blows it takes to penetrate the fat and kill the seal.

Kicking was very simple. Some sealers, because it was fast, preferred to kick a baby seal in the face, roll it over on its back, and cut its throat. This method was not used on adult seals because they can give painful bites, and a hooded seal could probably sever a leg.

Shooting was reserved for most of the adults. The reason for this was unless the seals stay to defend their young, the hunters cannot get close to the mature seals: the seals would escape down an airhole, or through a fault in the ice called a *lead*.

The object of shooting was to disable the adult seal before it could escape. Hunters would then rush in and club it to death. They would also shoot seals in the water hoping for a killing shot, in which case the animal floated to the surface. If it wasn't killed it escaped wounded beneath the ice. Seal hunters freely admitted that for every seal they were killing and recovering they were wounding four or five others. It was not unusual to see blood bubbling in the air-holes where the wounded seals had escaped. Sometimes an injured mother seal would struggle back onto the ice to die beside her wimpering, hungry baby.

Drowning usually took place on the north shore of the Gulf. There, the seals were trapped in nets or specially constructed traps close to shore and held under water until they drowned. Adult seals can normally stay under water for 20 minutes, but when *held* under water may be able to live for one half-hour or longer.

"Longlining" was the most terrible way of all to take seals. A cruelly sharp, baited hook was lowered into the water, and the unfortunate seal that swallowed the cutting hook was left to strangle in its own blood after perhaps hours of desperate struggle in the cold, dark waters

15

of the Gulf.

The killing of the young took place in full sight of the mothers who thrust their heads out of the water to watch with large, anxious eyes. Sometimes a mother seal would call to her baby as the hunter approached. Who could tell whether or not the females realized what was going on? But who cared, anyway? A busy hunter might kill as many as 125 seals in a day and had little time to worry about the sensitivities of mother seals.

After the young were slaughtered, and this took long agonized days with the females creeping back to the bleeding carcasses of their young at night, the hunters turned their attention to the adults.

The few hooded seals in the Gulf suffered a terrible fate if sighted by the hunters. The hooded seal is a different species from the harp seal, but the two herd in the same general vicinity. Male and female hooded seals will defend their young to the death. The baby hooded seal with its short-haired coat, blue on the back and white on the belly, fetched a premium price and the vanishing subherd of hooded seals in the Gulf were shown no mercy.

When a male, female, and baby hooded seal were sighted in a family group, the hunters moved in as a team of at least two. If no rifle were available, one man would thrust his hook and spiked gaff down the throat of the attacking adult while the other hunter would beat the huge animal over the head until it died. The male hooded seal inflates a bladder-like bag over his head when angry, and killing him was a long, desperate business. After killing the adults, the hunters quickly despatched the single pup.

When the ships and aircraft finally carried the killers from the Gulf of St. Lawrence, in 1964, the ice glowed a dull red from the spilled blood. And over 100,000 intelligent, and graceful animals had been pitilessly killed.

In 1964 much of this had been faithfully recorded by the team from *Artek Films* of Montreal. When the film was shown in French-speaking Canada, a storm of protest followed; and there was an even greater reaction from Europeans, after a showing of part of the film on television by Dr. Bernhard Grzimek, Director of the Frankfurt Zoo and a world-famous conservationist. Thousands of bitter protests were lodged with Canadian embassies abroad, and an alarmed Canadian Government suddenly realized it was responsible for the *world's cruellest and bloodiest hunt.*

Frantic interdepartmental memos must soon have established that the seals are migratory animals. They came under federal jurisdiction, not provincial. And that the gentleman responsible for the conduct of the seal hunt was the then Canadian Minister of Fisheries, the Honorable H. J. Robichaud.

What a tragedy this turned out to be for the seals! Mr. Robichaud acted, I believe, in an incredible way. Using all the government machinery at his disposal he sought to discredit those who opposed the seal hunt. Evidence that, in my opinion, would be rejected in any court of justice was presented as hard, proven fact. The people and parliament were misled, and the sealing industry, chuckling up its sleeve, would make only those improvements that did not interfere with profits.

A meeting between Canadian Government officials and the sealing industry was planned for the late spring of 1964, in order to draft regulations for the 1965 season, and Moncton, New Brunswick, was chosen as the location. I happened to be the Executive-Secretary of the New Brunswick SPCA and, as the meeting was to be held in my "territory", I was asked by the Canadian Federation of Humane Societies to attend as an SPCA observer. Although I did not know it at the time, this was to be a watershed in my life. I was to become what newspapers came to call a *crusader.*

Moncton is a small New Brunswick city on the banks of the Peticodiac River, a pleasant, tree-shaded community

17

of mixed English and French background. Planning the beating to death of thousands of helpless animals seemed very much out of place.

The rather grandly labeled Canadian Atlantic Sealing Meeting was held in the Federal Building on Main Street, on May 20th. And after various wrong turnings I found the right room. (I am the type of person who habitually pushes on doors marked "pull", and my passage through the building was marked by a trail of strained door-hinges.) The meeting was chaired by Dr. W. H. Needler, Deputy Minister of Fisheries. A heavy-set man of medium height, Dr. Needler held a key position. His advice to his Minister would be critical.

The room was crowded with people who make money from killing seals. The annual take of harp seals and hooded seals in the northwest Atlantic is, for the most part, handled by ships and aircraft operated by large commercial companies. And they were well represented at that meeting—the boat owners, the aircraft owners and the fur brokers. Strangely enough—or was it?—no actual seal-killer was there. Nor did anyone, that I could see, represent the land-based hunters—poor, hungry men who go out in small boats and brave the elements for a few dollars.

Nervous, and unsure of myself in a large meeting, I crept to a quiet corner hoping nobody would notice me. In fact, I was so successful that at the end of the meeting none of the sealing people knew that an official of a humane society had been present. At one point in the discussions, one of the men present had referred to humane society endorsement of various killing methods, and Dr. Needler glanced around the room obviously looking for me. Anxious not to be exposed as an animal-lover, I screwed my face into a savage leer, the sort of appearance I thought seal hunters habitually wore. Looking somewhat startled, Dr. Needler let the point pass.

18

My somewhat less than courageous attitude did pay dividends, however: I believe I heard the truth. I discovered that an over-capitalized sealing industry was intent on killing the last seal pup in order to get a return on its equipment, and that those who profited from the seals gave not one thought to their suffering.

Evidence presented to the meeting by Dr. D. E. Sergeant of the Fisheries Research Board of Canada clearly indicated that the seals, heavily hunted for centuries, were in a very bad way. Recent air surveys and catch statistics suggested the herds had been cut in half in the last ten years.

I looked around the room expecting to see some evidence of concern—somebody to say, "Poor devils. Give them a rest!" Hard, cold eyes stared Dr. Sergeant down. "So what, that leaves two million to go before we have to find other uses for our equipment." Unvoiced, that thought with its implied greed hung heavy in the stifling air of the small, crowded room.

When the discussion came round to killing-methods, everyone was an expert. Dull faces lit up; eyes and voices became eager. "Hit them on the nose." "No, no, hit them on the head." "My men say kicking is the quickest way." They were discussing the killing of helpless baby seals.

The same excitement appeared when these men discussed the killing of adults. One man admitted to flying over the seals in his light aircraft, shooting at them with a semi-automatic rifle aimed through an open window.

"I lost 60% of everything I hit,' he said, more in complaint at the unreasonableness of the seals who refused to die quickly than in apology for his brutal act.

It was Dr. Needler's turn. He let the meeting know that he did not believe it would be practical to ban sealing (smiles all round), but that the Government intended to meet popular demand. *"It is within the bounds of possibility, if the industry does not improve, that sealing will*

19

be banned." (An angry shuffling of feet from the meeting.) But Dr. Needler, with all his vast experience of public opinion and government, was being prophetic.

Off the coast of Canada, there are actually two herds of harp seals: the Gulf herd, so called because its members give birth and mate in the Gulf of St. Lawrence, and the Front herd, so called because its members give birth and mate in waters to the east of Labrador. It became abundantly clear at the meeting that decisive action could only be taken with regard to the Gulf herd. The Front herd, in international waters, an area where Canada could not assume total jurisdiction, must rely on the conscience of the world. A rare commodity.

The meeting dragged to its hot, stuffy conclusion. And at the end of it all, three points of future Government policy were evident. Sealers were to be licensed, the size of the club was to be regulated by law, and a quota was to be instituted so that the herd in the Gulf would not become extinct.

I drove to my home in Fredericton, New Brunswick, through 125 miles of glorious spring countryside. Wildlife abounded on every hand, and the coming summer had released the land from the grip of winter to turn it a delicate tint of green. But my thoughts were with the seals.

By the time I reached home, I had thought the problem through. There was one fundamental issue—*should the seal hunt continue or not?* I was not yet ready for a personal crusade, and decided to leave the choice to the Canadian Federation of Humane Societies. In my brief to them I posed two principles: the principle of conservation of seals and control of the industry (Conservation—Control), and the principle of *Abolition.*

In outlining both principles, I tried to be as objective as I could, although after the best part of a day with the sealing industry this was not easy. In my imagination I could feel the club smashing against the skulls of the young seals, and see the ice floes dripping blood into the blue ocean.

But there was a job to be done for the seals, and it appeared that, whatever the Federation decided, there would be a hunt in 1965. Thus, the immediate problem was that the animals should be given at least some relief.

I listed thirteen suggested regulations that would, in my opinion, effect some reasonable improvement. Only those suggestions that clearly coincided with the proposed Government regulations were given any serious consideration by the Minister of Fisheries. I was left to wonder whether my trip to Moncton had been of any value at all. *But it had—and Mr. Robichaud was to learn this, to his cost.*

Almost apologetically I outlined the principle of *Abolition.* I had never been for the abolition of anything before, and I was stepping into a new field that might see me severely attacked. Anyone suggesting that animals be given the right to live just because it was pleasant for them would be given a rough time. *Homo sapiens,* with his colossal conceit could hardly be expected to let that one by easily.

I said at the conclusion of my brief to the Federation, *"Seal hunting will always be a bloody and horrifying business for the seals."*

Under constant pressure from the Canadian Federation of Humane Societies, and alarmed by continuing public criticism, the Honorable H. J. Robichaud, Minister of Fisheries, in an interview in his office in Ottawa on October 14th, 1964, offered to take three representatives of the Canadian Humane Movement to the seal hunt in 1965. Mr. Robichaud had made the decision that was to torment his few remaining years in politics. *I was one of the three.*

CHAPTER THREE

A Trip to see Seals

THE men chosen to view the annual Canadian bloodletting were Mr. Tom Hughes, General Manager of the Ontario Humane Society (one of Canada's provincial groups), Mr. Jacques Vallée, General Manager of the Canadian Society for the Prevention of Cruelty to Animals (which operates as the Province of Quebec SPCA), and myself. Tom Hughes never reached the ice in 1965.

The slaughter was due to start March 11th, and I suggested to the Department of Fisheries, which was organizing the SPCA observations, that we should assemble somewhere close to the hunt a couple of days before the opening. My idea was rejected and I was told to be available to go to Prince Edward Island (P.E.I.) on March 13th. *This was crazy.*

P.E.I., located in the southwest corner of the Gulf of St. Lawrence, is Canada's smallest Province. Summer sees the island a veritable paradise with green fields sloping gently to warm, sandy beaches. Tourists crowd its narrow roads. But winter shows the island in another form. Cold fogs sweep in from the Gulf, snow storms block the roads and native islanders are not fooling when they say, "Prince Edward Island in the winter is a good place to be *from*."

We were to fly to the hunt, and I could see us trapped by winter fog while the seaborne hunters, indifferent to weather conditions, destroyed the seal herd. Events were to prove my fears well-grounded. In two and a half days the hunters destroyed 50,000 baby seals, all that were allowed under the new quota; not till March 13th was I called and told to proceed to P.E.I. By that time, the hunt had ended, and the seals had lost a year.

The question is: did Mr. Robichaud deliberately time events to prevent the SPCA team from observing the hunt? Did he want a *free* year in which to make improvements? Dr. David E. Sergeant, who had been at the Canadian Atlantic Sealing Meeting, was an expert on the seal hunt; he worked for Mr. Robichaud. Dr. Sergeant must have known how many hunters, ships, and aircraft were standing ready for the kill. He would have been able to calculate, almost to the minute, how long it would take the hunters to kill 50,000 baby seals. He could have advised his Minister; yet Mr. Robichaud kept the SPCA team on the mainland until it was too late to do its job. *Was this done with the deliberate intention of frustrating the Canadian Humane Movement?* Mr. Robichaud may have felt he needed his free year.

He got it, and ultimately it will cost some 100,000 seals. The hunt will end, but one year later than it otherwise would have if I had been given 1965.

Jacques Vallée and I met on P.E.I., on March 13th, and decided to go out to the ice floes even though the hunt was over. We were simple tourists, anxious to see seals. Tom Hughes had decided to stay home as there was no chance of doing the job for which the team had been organized.

Stanley Dudka was the fisheries officer in charge of enforcing the new seal-protection regulations. A tall, quiet, well-spoken man, Stanley acted as our guide.

Flying over the ice with Stanley, I looked down on a wonderland. Ice floated on the ocean, stretching as far as the eye could see. A crazy, patchwork pattern, each floe different, yet each floe the same. Smooth and flat, the ice chunks were jammed together by wind and sea and each had crumpled edges that formed a crown of jagged ice. Some floes were large enough to land an aircraft on, and indeed, some bore the tracks of the ski-equipped light aircraft used by the airborne hunters. Others were so small that a man could not hope to stand on them. In places the floes had separated into *leads*, exposing the cold, blue waters of the Gulf.

We flew on and on, suspended in a huge blue globe, and surrounded by occasional puffs of cloud, creamy white and gently soft.

Our helicopter turned and dipped, and there in the distance were small black shapes on the ice. We swept lower and saw the seals scattering into the water at our approach. With a roar of increased engine power the huge craft settled softly into a whirling cloud of snow. I climbed out.

The ice was covered with fresh snow and I could walk easily. There was just a gentle feeling of motion and I might almost have been on land. Leaving the rest of the party I walked across to the jagged, broken ice at the edge of our large floe. I sat down alone and felt the silence as something tangible. The tableau of the ice, every shade of blue, surrounded me save where, on my left, an open *lead* had tiny wavelets lapping against the floes. I could see the jagged undersurface of a nearby expanse of ice reaching down, deep into the waters. I judged the ice to be some four feet thick.

Out of the corner of my eye I caught movement. I hurried across the broken ice to the next floe, and was captivated. The eyes of a baby harp seal seem to reach out and insinuate themselves into one's very soul. Huge, dark, inquisitive, happy, sad, seemingly all at the same time. They give to the baby seal an identity few other animals can match.

The little fellow I was watching was about ten days old

and weighed some 50 pounds. His long white coat stood out around his body in a puff of fur. About the size of a year-old human baby, he wriggled towards me uttering low cries. Suddenly, sensing I was not mother he stopped, looked alarmed, but when I did not move decided to ignore me.

I watched, fascinated, absorbing the beauty of the total scene. The brilliant sky, blue tipped ice with its tumbled crown, the murmuring water and the beautiful animals. Nature was never more in harmony.

I moved towards the little seal, and again the alarm. He drew his head into his shoulders in a way that I later learned was common to these animals and stopped breathing. His eyes closed tightly and tears pressed out between the lids. He might have been dead. I touched him: no reaction. I sat down beside him and gently stroked him. Slowly life returned, and he opened his eyes. Blinking, he looked at me. I saw the black button of his nose twitch as oxygen flooded into his lungs. Then, with a cry, he wriggled away.

The immediate spell was broken and I readied my camera. I had work to do for these little fellows. Others had to care about them—others who would never see a seal and who could never experience, other than through me, the wonder of these moments. I rapidly used a roll of film, and one picture was outstanding. A full-face shot that I have used for the past four years. My little friend with his beautiful eyes and black button nose.

I wandered from floe to floe, sometimes on my own, sometimes accompanied by one of the party who had come with me to the ice. I saw dozens of baby seals and adults. I was in a wonderland—the incredibly beautiful, harp seal nursery of the Gulf of St. Lawrence.

My first breathless excitement was replaced by curiosity. I looked more closely at the seals. The babies were shaped like an exclamation mark without the dot. They moved with a side-to-side wriggling motion, at the same time pulling themselves forward with their front flippers—vestigial arms that still bore five fingernails. Their hind flippers were like two hands crossed in prayer, and again, the five fingernails. I can well imagine why many biologists consider sea mammals the most advanced form of non-human life.

The adults were superbly adapted to their cold environment. Thick hair covered a tough, leathery skin. Underneath the skin a thick layer of blubber protected them from cold. The reason for the name "harp" seal was obvious. On each side of the body was the black outline of a harp. They moved differently from the babies, at least they did on the ice. They "humped" themselves forward with a movement that started from the hind flippers and flowed through their bodies to the neck. They could barely use their front flippers as an aid to movement as each seal was so fat through the body that these flippers hardly reached the ice. Aside from the black harp marks and other black spots distributed over their bodies, the adults were a creamy white. Occasionally, I would see a young adult that was a greyish blue with no harp marks, just scattered dark spots.

In the water the adults were poetry. I sat beside an area of open water and watched them swim. Fantastic! First, they would stand seemingly upright in the water, and look at me, all fifty or so of them. Then, as one, they would flip over and swim across the *lead*. As they flowed over the surface of the water I struggled to capture the sight in words.

"Like ears of corn rippling in a summer breeze," I said aloud. A startled young seal, close to my feet, looked up and barked quickly.

Suddenly, a dark head bobbed up from a hole in the ice. Mother was objecting. I moved away, lay down, and watched. Again, the dark head appeared in the hole in the ice kept open by her constant movement. She looked carefully around. Lying still on the ice, I must have resembled a rather portly, mother seal. With a gigantic heave she hauled herself out of the water. Then baby cried shrilly and moved towards her. Their noses met. "O.K., you're mine," she seemed to say.

Captivated, I watched and watched. I close my eyes, and four years later I can still see that scene in every detail.

We left the harp seals and the helicopter carried us to another patch of dark shapes on the ice—but different shapes to the harp seals. Twisting into crescents, these animals turned to look up at us: and they did not scatter as our helicopter settled to the ice in its usual flurry of blown snow. These were brave hooded seals, mysterious and magnificent.

Surrounded by jagged blocks of ice was the "nest" of a single hooded seal family—male, female, and one pup. The ice in the nest, worn smooth by their huge bodies, was slick and blue. There was blood on the surrounding snow. Apparently the mother had only recently given birth and the umbilical cord of her baby was red and wet. Both the male and female were grey-blue in color with many dark, leopard-like spots. The male, weighing some 900 pounds, bared his huge, yellow teeth. Angry, a "hood" of loose skin inflated on his head, and his nostrils flared red. As we approached, he roared and moved towards us. We moved back, fearful of the extent of his territorial defence. But he was content to keep us outside the jagged ice surrounding his home.

I looked at the female. About one-third smaller than her mate, she lay bodily across her baby, her eyes worried looking and her massive jaws open. Without the hood of the male she looked less fierce—but all mother.

The young hood had a short coat of stiff hair, blue on the head and back and white underneath. Although conforming in general detail to the baby harp seal, the baby hooded seal was less beautiful.

With my camera I recorded on film this wonderful scene. Lacking a telephoto lense, I would move into the nest area, crouch down and wait for the male to charge me, which he always did. Then, when he was four or five feet away I would take my picture, turn, and run into the broken ice. It seemed as though he really did not want to hurt me, because when I broke and ran he would invariably stop. Animals rarely make total war: they content themselves with limited objectives, I thought.

The mother seal kept her defensive posture over her young one, daring anyone, including the male, whom she repulsed with angry nips, to go too close. Suddenly, the helicopter clattered into life and lifted into the air. Blowing snow enveloped the seals. The male, shaken, broke and fled. The female, in one of the bravest acts I have ever seen, kept her position. Lifting her head and shoulders into the air, she tried to tear the huge machine from the sky. I looked at her in admiration. Few animals would have shown such courage: and the hunters beat them to death.

Not wanting to disturb them further, I moved on. I walked across a medium-sized floe towards a lead and was startled to see two male hoods suddenly lunge out of the water onto the ice. One hundred yards apart to start with they ran—and "ran" is the only word I can use, although they moved over the ice in the same fashion as harp seals —towards each other. Expecting a ferocious battle as their hoods were inflated, I watched apprehensively. But they passed each other and disappeared into the water. What on earth possessed them? They had actually brushed in passing.

My next experience was to be a look at the other side of the seal's life, a look at the aircraft and men who hunt them. Our helicopter circled a huge ice floe on which were resting two light, single-engined aircraft. They had landed on skis and their tracks spread over the snow.

I came across a group of hunters who had been shooting adults. While the fisheries officer who accompanied me spoke to them, I wandered over to look at the aircraft. Built to carry the pilot up front and one passenger in a rear seat, each was a versatile and handy machine. The passenger seats had been taken out and the rear compartments lined with plywood. Blood-soaked, the very wood seemed to echo the tragedy of the hunt.

Breaking all regulations the pilots, I was told, would cram two, and sometimes three, hunters into a space meant for one and, grossly overloaded, would head for the ice. Similarly, when taking a load of pelts back to land the machine would be overloaded. Sometimes these aircraft could barely stagger into the air, and the accident rate was high. In 1965, several machines crashed and two men were killed. But *they* made a choice. The *seals* had no say: they were unwilling victims in the brutal killing.

I left the aircraft and walked over to the hunters. Some were carrying light, semi-automatic rifles firing ·22 caliber bullets—pea-shooters, and no weapon to stop 500 pounds of escaping seal.

I questioned them and was told they expected to lose four of five wounded seals for every one they shot and recovered. This high rate of cripples did not seem to bother them. It was almost as if the seals were inanimate, had no feelings. Certainly these men had no concern for the seals.

They described to me how they hunted the seals. Creeping through broken ice they would approach a group of adult seals basking in the sun, near an air hole or *lead*. Taking care to keep downwind of the animals they would sometimes get within 200 feet or so, then, at a signal, they would leap to their feet. A couple of men would blaze away with their light, semi-automatic rifles in an effort to disable as many seals as possible before they escaped. And seals move fast when frightened. Then the men with clubs would move in and beat injured animals to death. I looked at the clubs. Blood-red, with bits of bone and flesh sticking to them. A great way to earn a dollar, I thought.

Several of the men wore gas-station uniforms, and I learned that most of the hunting group worked on automobiles for a living. The "boss" of the group was a preacher. I asked him if he said a prayer for the seals as he killed them. He didn't answer.

Because of the weight of the heavy adult pelts, the men were scraping the thick layer of blubber from them before loading them in the aircraft. I watched one man stretch out a skin, hair-side to the ice, and scrape away at the blubber with a garden hoe sharpened to a good edge. It seemed so incongruous.

On my own, I covered the recent hunt area and was shocked. The water in many of the *leads* and air holes was red. And with no seals to keep them open the air holes were freezing over. Blood-red ice. Like colored ice in a cocktail ... I could only imagine the suffering that was, even then, going on underneath my feet. What right had man to treat these beautiful and intelligent animals in such a manner? Could money really be a good enough excuse?

Troubled, I sat on the ice to think it through. I live in a society where almost any torturing of animals is "go" if some human makes money from it. Our animal, anti-cruelty laws only recognize suffering as criminal in the most exceptional circumstances. If someone makes a dollar, pain becomes necessary and even morally acceptable. I could not help but think that society had a few screws loose somewhere.

Stanley Dudka walked across to me, and together we continued our search of the area.

Suddenly, I saw a seal lying beside an air-hole. I had not been able to get very close to an adult harp before, and this seemed like a perfect opportunity. Stanley and I crept, as silently as we could, towards the great animal. After a few seconds we sensed something was wrong and slowly stood up. Quietly we walked the remaining few yards to the seal. It was a female, we later learned, and very dead. Obviously, it had been wounded, escaped beneath the ice, then had heaved its suffering body onto the floe to die in cold loneliness.

I remembered a story told by Dr. Harry Lillie, the famous Scottish surgeon who had worked hard and long for the Newfoundland seals. Dr. Lillie told of finding an adult seal injured by rifle fire. Ignoring her strong teeth he lay beside her on the ice stroking her head and talking to her. After a few minutes, the lovely animal put her head on his chest and he comforted her until she died.

There had been no Dr. Lillie to comfort this poor creature. She had died alone.

I left the ice that day out of tune with the beauty that still surrounded me. I felt ashamed to be a human being.

Why is it man can be so callous, I later thought, not only to animals but to other humans as well? I decided then that *cruelty* in any form, to any creature, was part of a sickness that might some day choke our civilization unless recognized as evil and eliminated.

Never again would I accept, unchallenged, the premise that man held complete dominion over animals. The seals had paid too high a price for such childish thinking. Man holds no dominion granted by heaven. We are merely able to inflict our will on defenceless creatures, and one day we may pay a terrible price.

Perhaps part of that price is being paid in our growing indifference to the suffering of our fellow man. The hardness of soul that is a prerequisite for watching unmoved the suffering of man could start in watching the suffering of helpless animals and doing nothing about it.

But the day was to end with excitement and hope. Jack and Jill were waiting to be discovered.

CHAPTER FOUR

Jack and Jill

THE helicopter taking us back home from the ice floes to Prince Edward Island droned steadily on its way. The late afternoon sky was steely grey, and stray flights of snow whipped by the windows. I dozed fitfully. In spite of my thick socks and high boots my feet were cold. In fact, I had felt cold all day due mainly to the fact that I was not very well dressed for tramping around on ice floes. Most of my clothes were borrowed and were either too big or too small.

P.E.I. at last. We swept into an area used by airborne hunters, and I learned more of this highly sophisticated side of the sealing operation. Light, fixed-wing aircraft and helicopters lift men out to the seals, almost always hunting for babies, because these pelts provide more value per pound than do the adult pelts. With weight a constant problem the aircraft operators tend to stay with the young seals. Having got a group of hunters out, sometimes as many as six, the individual aircraft would then ferry the pelts back and forth to the nearest point of land where Canadian Government inspectors counted the skins so that when all commercial groups had killed approximately 50,000 baby seals in Gulf Area 2, the main breeding area, the hunt by these people could be stopped. (Land-based hunters, however, were subject to no such regulations, and if the seals

32

came close enough to land there was nothing to limit the kill. In fact, I was told that on one occasion the seals came very close to the Magdalen Islands, and even children raced out to the ice after school to kill young seals. It might be added that Magdalen Island children were not the only ones to kill seals. Often, when the ice floes come close to Nova Scotia as they race through the Cabot Straits, daring Nova Scotian schoolchildren will go out from the shore jumping from clamper to clamper [the name they give the ice floes]. Woe betide any baby seal they find. Lacking clubs, they are known to punch or kick the animal in the nose, believing that this is an effective way of despatching them.)

The aircraft were lined up in rows, perhaps twenty-five altogether. Canvas covers were wrapped around the engines to keep out the driving snow. Here and there the plastic bubble of a small helicopter stood out in contrast to the angular lines of the conventional aircraft. Red, 45-gallon drums of gasoline were scattered throughout the impromptu airfield in the snow. I was amazed at the casual way men were refueling aircraft. Lighted cigarettes dangled from their lips in contravention of normal safety procedures.

A few yards from the aircraft stood the canvas tents used by the pilots and engineers—little havens of warmth where the rye-whisky flowed and the stories grew more colorful as the evening wore on.

Perhaps the majority of the pilots felt sorry for the seals, but their greed for experience and money is greater than their concern for animals, or people for that matter. For instance, Canadian regulations for the operation of light aircraft had been, I was told, largely ignored, and these regulations are framed with one purpose in mind—safety of aircraft and passengers.

As I stood there watching the local children chasing in and out of the rows of aircraft, I noticed two small white shapes some distance from me. For a moment I thought

33

they might be seals, but I quickly rejected that idea. No seals had come on land this year, although the folklore of P.E.I. records that seals did come ashore on the island one year—when there was no ice in the Gulf.

Then, unable to contain my curiosity any longer, I walked over. Surprise—utter and complete—the white shapes were baby seals.

I questioned the children who were standing near-by. I was told pilots had brought the seals back to land. Then they had tired of their playthings and had given them to some children. I was shocked and angry. These unfortunate young animals, some five days old, had been callously left to starve to death.

I was faced with a real problem. All instincts said "save the seals", but logic said, "destroy them: why bother about two more when 50,000 have just been killed?" But that was the point. So many had been killed, so many had been shown no mercy by man. Perhaps now was the time to prove that some men can consider even the lives of two hungry little seals of value, although a stone's throw away the bloody little carcasses of 50,000 of their relatives lay frozen on the ice, mute testimony to one of man's most base instincts—greed. I decided to try to save them. A faint prophetic stirring in my mind told me that I had made the right decision.

I loaded the two seals into the waiting Government helicopter, and we lifted into the air on our errand of mercy. Suddenly, everyone in the cabin was smiling. The fisheries officers had watched so much killing in the past few days that saving these two babies suddenly became important.

My two young friends objected loudly to their new surroundings, but their loudest cries were drowned out by the deafening roar of the helicopter's huge, air-cooled engine. Shouting, I discussed with the fisheries officers the possibility of returning the two seals to the herd which still

34

lay off P.E.I. I dropped that idea when I was told that there was only one chance in a quarter of a million of reaching the right mothers; and no seals, other than the natural mothers, would take my two little orphans.

We landed at our motel in Alberton, a small town in western P.E.I., and I carried the two baby seals to the snow-covered lawn in front of the main building.

Soon I was surrounded by a crowd of onlookers and everyone enthused over Jack and Jill, as I had instinctively christened my two charges. The two baby seals, hungry, cried pitifully. One of the fisheries officers, anxious perhaps to get rid of someone he must have thought a complete lunatic, offered to drive me to the nearest large town, Summerside, where I could rent a car to take me and the seals to my home in New Brunswick.

I stowed the seals carefully in the trunk of the fisheries department vehicle and headed along the bumpy road to Summerside. Jack and Jill were really the start of the movement to "Save the Seals". Through them I formed connections with the news media that would prove so valuable in the future. It is ironic that an employee of the Cabinet Minister who was to suffer such severe headaches over the seal hunt should be the individual who helped us on our way. But none of those involved, including me, realized this at the time. All we wanted to do was give two little animals a chance of life.

During the drive I listened intently for noises from the rear of the vehicle. Every bump brought me out in a sweat of apprehension in case the animals were hurt. I interpreted every noise from a laboring rear axle or creaky old transmission as a seal crying in fear or pain. I must have behaved like an old mother hen, and my driver was probably glad to reach Summerside and be rid of me.

But there was a problem to be dealt with before I could transfer my seals from the fisheries vehicle to a rent-a-car. I had no money and I had left my driver's license at home.

Normally these two items are vital for car renting. Determined to get a car for my dash to the ferry which crossed the Northumberland Straits every few hours, and in order to complete the subsequent trip home, I was inspired. Somehow or other I convinced the manager of the car rental agency that I was honest and that he should wave normal requirements. I felt it somewhat unwise to mention that his new car would have two rather wet baby seals as rear-seat passengers.

Slipping and sliding on the ice, I transferred the seals from one vehicle to the other, and in fair imitation of an escaping bank robber gunned my car out of town. I wanted to prevent the manager looking in to see what had been placed on the rear seat of his car. I did, however, have a hastily constructed plan ready if such an eventuality occurred before I could flee the area. I was prepared to claim that the two wooly white bundles in the car were earmuffs for elephants.

Fast driving over slippery roads got me to the early evening ferry, and I was able to eat for the first time that day. I knew the two seals must also be very hungry, and I tried to locate some baby bottles, but with no success.

It was dark and cold when I arrived at Cape Tormentine, the New Brunswick terminus of the ferry, and I was not looking forward to the long trip home. Alone and tired, it would be hell.

Between me and my home in Fredericton lay Moncton, and in Moncton was an animal shelter operated by the Moncton SPCA. I telephoned that truly merciful woman, Mrs. J. E. Hoover, President of the group.

"Will you help me feed two baby seals?"

"Of course," she said, with no surprise in her voice.

"Fine, have two baby bottles and milk ready at the shelter, and I'll be there in about one and a half hours," I said.

I can still remember that journey. I was becoming increasingly worried about the seals. I believed they must have been without food for days, and frequent glances in the back of the car did nothing to reassure me. They lay on the rear seat hardly moving, and looking very weak. I cursed those who had brought them back to land and abandoned them.

Aching with tiredness I drove into the shelter yard and was met by Mrs. Hoover, complete with bottles and milk. A real animal lover in the best sense of the word, Mrs. Hoover was ready to have a go at feeding the seals. Quite how one feeds harp seal pups we did not know, and events that night were to prove that, in fact, it was beyond our wit to discover.

I carried the seals, one by one, into the small kitchen of the shelter, and in a few minutes two sorry little white bundles lay on the linoleum-covered floor. I tentatively knelt down in front of the seal we later called Jill and offered her a bottle, fully expecting her to suck heartily. Two large dark eyes, tear filled, looked at me, but no pink mouth opened hungrily to seize the proffered nipple. Instead, with a plaintive cry, she turned away from me. Obviously, I did not resemble a fat mother-seal.

I looked at Mrs. Hoover. She didn't look like a mother seal either. But she was a woman, and long experience with animals had taught me that animals recognize a difference in the sex of humans and that some creatures have a decided preference, one way or the other. Admitting defeat rather grudgingly, because I rather fancied myself as a handler of baby seals, I gave her the bottle.

Mrs. Hoover knelt down in front of Jill. She received the same response I had got.

"O.K., let's try Jack," I said.

Jack, with an almost human gesture of contempt, turned his back on us. We weren't going to be beaten. I knelt astride Jill to hold her immobile, and Mrs. Hoover again offered her the bottle. Still she refused. Back to Jack ...

same response. The two seals looked at each other ... plaint-
ively. Somewhat naively we tried giving them milk in a
saucer, although anything more unlike the nipple of a
mother seal is hard to imagine. Negative results.

Searching my mind desperately for a solution to the
problem, I decided to imitate a mother seal. I had seen a
picture of a female seal feeding her baby, and the nipple
appeared to be in the general area of her stomach. I lay
down beside the two animals, braced the bottom of the
bottle firmly against my stomach, and thrust it, rather in-
vitingly I thought, in their general direction. Mrs. Hoover
looked on in amused despair, and the seal babies looked
at me as though I was mad. Sheepishly, I clambered to
my feet.

"Mrs. Hoover, we're beat. It's time I headed for home,"
I said. "Joan (my wife) will have the answer to this problem." How wrong I was!

The journey to Fredericton took about two and a half
hours and covered some 115 miles. It was a long drive
through snow-covered fields and forests. Only a few communities and isolated farms dotted the highway. In spite
of the cold and snow a Canadian winter's night is beautiful.
Clusters of stars gleamed icily in the clear night sky, and
a full moon, dipping occasionally behind the trees on a
hilltop, threw branches into lace-like silhouettes. I could
have enjoyed the drive as I had drunk several cups of
coffee in Moncton and was feeling less tired, but I was
constantly nagged by the thought of the two hungry animals
in the rear of the car.

Home at last, but late, late at night. Joan was expecting
me, but certainly not two baby seals. I had no qualms,
however: I knew she would be delighted with them. With
a seal under each arm I marched into the living room,
struggling with reluctant doorknobs on the way. I knew
my entrance with even one seal would cause a sensation,
and sensation I got, but not quite what I was expecting.

My four-year-old daughter, Toni, and eight-year-old son, Nicky, had been allowed to stay up to hear tales about the seals. Toni was absolutely horrified at the sight of the two furry bundles, and burst into frightened tears. She had been having nightmares recently about white goats, and must have thought they had finally come to get her. Joan eventually quieted her down, and I proudly displayed my find.

A quick run-down on events leading up to the moment, and it was back to baby bottles.

With all the skill of raising two babies, and a real love for animals at her call, Joan tried to feed them. I was horrified ... the pair just would not suck. They would not lap; they would not swallow when we tried to tip it down their throats; in fact, they would not do anything but look miserable and hungry. They had even given up crying, presumably from exhaustion. We struggled for about one and a half hours until we were as weak as the seals. Then we gave up and went to bed for a few hours.

Very early we were hard at it with the bottles, and with the same negative results. We needed help.

Dr. Elizabeth Simpson, a young English veterinarian, had a new practice in Fredericton. She was a brilliant animal doctor and a good friend. We phoned her and she promised to come down as soon as she could.

In the meantime, what? Murray Kinloch was a director of the New Brunswick SPCA. A Scottish professor of English, he was always ready to help with animal problems. We reached him on the telephone.

For a long moment he considered my story; then said, "I remember reading about a chap in England who specializes in raising baby seals. Why don't you try to contact him through the United Kingdom R.S.P.C.A.?"

"What's his name?" I asked.

"I don't know," was the helpful reply.

I dialed the telephone operator in Fredericton; and, not

wanting to divulge my unusual request to a local girl, I asked for the United Kingdom Overseas Operator in Montreal. Within seconds I was through.

Not at all sure of the reception I would get, I told my story of two baby seals that would not suck from a bottle. I explained that there was a man in England who knew how to feed seals and that it might be possible to contact him through the Royal Society for the Prevention of Cruelty to Animals in London. I had no names or telephone numbers to offer her, but in an appeal to her motherhood I held the mouthpiece of the telephone in front of a whimpering Jack and Jill.

"Please hang up your telephone, sir, and I'll call you back when I have the information you require."

Incredibly, within a few minutes the young lady in Montreal had called me back and I was speaking to Chief Inspector Charles Morrison of the RSPCA. Inspector Morrison lived in King's Lynn, Norfolk, England, and had wide experience of rearing baby seals washed up on the east coast.

It seems that baby seals are reluctant to suck at anything but the nipples of mother seals. Even baby bottles presented to them by SPCA executives lying full length on the floor and held at the level of the stomach do not turn them on. They must be "intubated", and plain milk is not good enough.

Intubated. The word frightened me. I had heard of enemas, and it seemed to me there might be some close relationship. Cautiously, I asked Inspector Morrison to explain.

Someone had to thrust a long plastic tube with a funnel at one end down the throat of the seal—not the funnel end. Following this complicated operation, which I was sure was going to be resisted strongly by the animal concerned, a special diet with a base of whale oil had to be poured into the animal's stomach *via* the funnel and tube.

Living, as I do, on the east coast of Canada, I assumed that whale oil was easily obtainable, but the two seals were to come close to death before I managed to lay my hands on this essential part of their diet. At that time I was not aware of the terrible cruelty involved in the taking of whales, so I was not faced with the dilemma of using a product of great suffering or sacrificing Jack and Jill.

Joan, who was to nurse Jack and Jill devotedly for two and a half weeks, had been listening on the extension phone. Our immediate problem had been solved. We knew how to get food into them; but what food? What could we use as a substitute for whale oil? We decided to call our friend, Dr. Elizabeth Simpson. Liz would know. We called her, and she did know.

Until the whale oil arrived, Jack and Jill should be fed a mixture of butter, milk, eggs, vitamins and antibiotics. I went to the local store to buy pounds of butter, quarts of milk, and dozens of eggs. All of this was done at a run, because we estimated the two seals had been without food for five days and might be very close to death.

Having got the first batch of food ready, we faced the job of getting tubes down throats. Fortunately, Liz had arrived and the operation proceeded smoothly enough. Joan knelt on the floor with a seal between her legs and held its head while Liz thrust the tube, well-greased, into the waiting stomach.

Only two problems presented themselves. Jack would not open his mouth to accept the tube and his jaws had to be pried open with careful fingers; and both animals, unused to such handling, evacuated their bowels over the legs of the "restrainer". In the two and a half weeks that Joan cared for the two animals, we were never able to get Jack to open his mouth voluntarily. The other problem was solved by wrapping each animal in a sheet before proceeding to feed it.

41

We had a big job on our hands, and some kind of systematic procedure had to be worked out.

The basement of my house is divided in two. At that time one half was occupied by a young married couple,[1] and the rest was divided into two rooms, one of which I used as an office. We decided to keep the seals in my office and cleared the furniture out. In order to approximate as closely as we could the temperature seals normally live in, the heat to the room, supplied by central heating in the winter, was turned off and a small window left wide open. The cold, March wind did keep the temperature down, but drove my home heating bill up.

Liz decided that the seals had to be fed four times a day, and that all the instruments used to prepare and administer the food were to be sterilized for each feeding, and for each seal. This, of course, was to reduce the chance of infection and, if that occurred, cross-infection. Joan, on her own, just could not cope with the two animals, and we turned for help to a neighbor, Rita Martinson. Rita, an Englishwoman, was very fond of animals. Neglecting housework, Joan and Rita devoted their time to nursing baby seals.

By this time the local press had discovered Jack and Jill. Stories that were to turn the two animals into international celebrities were appearing in newspapers throughout the world. The best were written by Yvonne Burgess, and were carried by United Press International. Yvonne was in almost daily contact with us from her headquarters in Halifax, Nova Scotia; and when she heard that the seals were straining the meagre resources of both the Davies family and the New Brunswick SPCA, she helped launch the "Save the Seals" Fund. Her headline read—"Got A Dime for a Cup of Whale Oil?" Within a few days, over $500 came in from various parts of Canada. At that point we called a halt to any further fund raising believing that

---

[1] They took to their new neighbours well.

this was sufficient money to care for the seals We never lost contact with these first well-wishers, however, and they were to form the nucleus for an expanded "Fund" that would take on the task of ending the seal hunt in the Gulf of St. Lawrence.

During this period I had been trying everywhere to buy whale oil—but no results. I had the feeling that some whaling companies also had an interest in sealing, and were not about to draw attention to baby seal hunting by helping us keep Jask and Jill alive. It was in their best interest to have the two little animals tidily dead, and out of the way.

We were having trouble getting the butter to mix satisfactorily with the milk even though we were using an emulsifier, so Liz suggested we substitute full cream for butter. This solved the mixing problem, but the seals, who should have been gaining some three pounds in weight every day, were slowly losing ground. Jill developed bronchitis, and both seals suffered from persistent enteritis. Whale oil was desperately needed.

Back to RSPCA Inspector Morrison. Another telephone call brought from him a promise of two gallons of whale oil to be shipped to us by air-express. We waited and waited.

Much of Canada was holding its breath. Would the baby seals survive? And still no whale oil. At this point Air Canada stepped in, locating the oil in London, giving the two rather greasy cans V.I.P. treatment, and whisking them to Fredericton airport.

We had become very attached to the two little animals, and suffered with them as they struggled to survive on their unnatural diet. When I received the call telling me the whale oil had arrived I rushed over to the airport, signed the necessary documents, and within minutes of my arriving home the two babies had been fed a meal that included a proper portion of whale oil. Flushed with

43

success, Joan, Rita, Liz, and I sat down to a well-earned beer.

Apart from the very real problem of looking after seals, we were having to cope with dozens of callers at our back door, all of them anxious for the seals and wanting to see them. Although we were delighted to see this interest in animals, sheer weight of numbers forced us to make a public appeal asking well-wishers not to call on us. The torrent slowed to a minor rush.

In retrospect, it is hard to believe the two seals caused Joan so much work she had no time or energy to cook meals, but it's true. For two and a half weeks the Davies' family existed on food hand-outs from friends, and "take-out" meals from a local restaurant, the last few of them paid for, when the cost became prohibitive to me, by the "Save the Seals" Fund on the prompt authorization of its directors. Liz, and her husband Peter, played a valiant part in this direction, not only providing the seals with constant veterinary attention, but bringing the occasional meal to feed the human part of the team.

In a typical day, Joan would get up early in the morning, see me off to Teacher's College where I was a student (I worked only part-time for the New Brunswick SPCA then), and Nicky off to school. Then she would face a dreadful mess in the basement. Jack and Jill were about as un-toilet-trained as it was possible to be, and would be swimming in seal droppings after a night of careening around my ex-office. This was bad enough, but the mixed stench of seal and whale-oil at close-quarters was unbelievable. Joan never complained.

Tip-toeing over the driest patches of floor she would wrap one or the other of the seals in a bedspread and carry it up two flights of stairs to the bathroom. Her passage through the house was hilarious. The seals never ceased objecting to being carried, and would struggle, nip, and roar all the way to the bath. Joan's efforts to avoid wildly

44

swinging rear flippers and still negotiate the stairs were a pantomime. Having got her seal to the bathroom, all was peace as she slipped him or her into a bath full of cold water.

Young as they were, Jack and Jill loved the water. They would swim and dive, roll, catch the water as it spouted out of the tap, and in spite of the small confines of the regular sized bath would manage to look exquisitely graceful.

Four-year-old Toni had lost her fear of seals by this time, and leaving her to push the two back into the water whenever they tried to get out of the bath, Joan would go downstairs to clean up the *seal room*. What a job! On weekends Nicky relieved Toni, and pushed seals back into the bath.

All bedsheets in the house had been called into service, and Joan's first job was using them to mop up the worst of the mess. Then buckets of hot water, disinfectant, and a scrubbing brush to get the floor and bottom halves of the walls clean, and germ-free. Extra scrubbing was required on the baseboards of the room because the seals used them as substitute mothers, and would spend much of the night sucking at them. Sometimes, late at night when all was quiet, we could hear them grunting and making little sucking noises as they worked away at the unyielding wood. I always felt especially sorry for them at such moments.

After the room was cleaned, Joan would put the soiled sheets and bedspreads into the washer. Then it was time to prepare their first feed of the day, which they received promptly at 10:00 a.m. A mixture of bottles, jugs, spoons, and tubes had to be thoroughly sterilized, because we were still fighting intestinal infection.

While the seal "formula" was being gently heated, Joan and one or both of the children would empty the bath, watch in delight as the seals tried to follow the water

45

down the drain, and finally dry the two animals. After that Joan would dry Toni,[2] who always managed to get as wet as Jack and Jill, and loved it. Then it was bedspreads again and back downstairs. Helped by Rita, who would have arrived by this time, Joan would begin the job of feeding. Jack never ceased refusing to open his mouth and prodding fingers were often painfully nipped. Jill was always more easy to fool. She would open her mouth (in a gesture common to females!) to roar, and this gave the "seal-feeders" a perfect opportunity to pop the long plastic tube inside. Pushing it into the waiting stomach was never a problem once the initial barrier of teeth was passed.

Both the seals would relax as the food flowed into them, presumably because a full-stomach felt good but, during the period we had them, they never seemed to realize that a plastic tube was the forerunner of a satisfied tummy. Perhaps we did not have them long enough for them to learn, although they went through dozens of feedings before they left.

After finishing their meal, Jack and Jill would immediately spend a little time sucking at baseboards, and Joan would be free to clean up any new mess they had made and finish her daily wash. The final task was the bathroom, always covered in short, white hair as the two seals moulted their initial baby coat.

Almost as soon as the 10:00 a.m. sequence was finished, it was time for the 2:00 p.m. struggle. The 6:00 p.m. and 10:00 p.m. baths and feedings saw me replacing Rita. Sometime around 11:00 p.m. at night Joan and I would be through with seals for the day and, bone-weary, would tumble into our sheetless and bedspreadless bed.

One day followed another in what had become a fascinating, but physically wearying routine. Looking back I can remember funny little incidents. The time Joan and Rita got the seals mixed up at feeding time and Jack

---

[2] Nicky, older, managed to keep reasonably dry.

received the best part of two dinners, causing him finally to resemble a fountain in some bizarre London square as the food gushed out of his mouth as fast as it was being poured in. Or the time that Jill, for some reason, started to eat sand when we put her out in our front garden for some fresh air.

When the seals started to gain about a pound a day in weight on their whale-oil diet, all of us involved faced the problem of where they would spend the rest of their lives. Joan and I would have loved to keep them with us, but had no facilities for properly caring for what would inevitably become two extremely large animals. And I couldn't imagine Joan continuing to carry them to and from the bath very much longer. In fact, if we delayed our move too long, I fully expected to see the seals carrying Joan to the bath as they got larger and more demanding!

We believed there were only two alternatives open to us. We could return the seals to the sea, or give them to a zoo.

I thought long and hard of returning them to the Gulf of St. Lawrence, but they'd had such a poor start and were still so much smaller and lighter than they should have been for their age that I felt sure if I did this they would be unable to cope with the challenging demands of nature and would die. A good zoo would offer them proper care and comfortable surroundings, and I believed a better chance for life. A zoo it would be.

Mr. Tom I. Hughes, General Manager of the Ontario Humane Society, had taken a personal interest in Jack and Jill and found a home for them at the City of Vancouver Zoo in British Columbia.

Again, Air Canada came to the rescue and offered to fly the two animals to Vancouver at no cost to the "Save the Seals" Fund and, with all the fanfare of a skillfully conducted Air Canada public relations campaign, the seals left for Vancouver late in March. Joan, Liz, and Rita

travelled with the seals as far as Montreal in order to clean
them up and give them a final feed and medical check-up
before the last, long leg of their journey to Vancouver.
Officials of the Canadian SPCA met our group at the airport and provided them with much-needed facilities. All in
all, it was a remarkable example of cooperation on the
part of the Humane Movement in Canada.

Mr. Alan Best, Zoo curator, very kindly wrote to me on
April 1st, 1965, saying that:

> "The two seals arrived in excellent condition and were
> escorted immediately to the aquarium where they were
> put into an enclosure with six inches of water.
> I had not expected them, being so young, to be seriously
> interested in water, but they loved it and rolled and
> played in it for 15 or 20 minutes before going to sleep.
> Obviously they delighted in the coolness of it after their
> long, hot journey.
> Within the next day or two the weaning process will be
> started, although they will be kept on the fish oil, milk
> formula for some time after they begin to take solid
> food.
> I must say that you have done an excellent job with
> them and I am most impressed."

Success and kind words—and to a great extent due to
Joan, Liz and Rita.

Jack died within six months, and Jill after a year at the
aquarium. Both from unknown causes. Was it worth it?
A lot of people lavished care, attention, and money on the
two animals during their brief life. Would it have been
wiser, or even perhaps kinder, to have killed them on the
shores of Prince Edward Island? It all depends on one's
point of view.

Initially I could not know that the seals would not live
a long and happy life. There *had* been too much killing;
it was time for compassion. Jack and Jill *did* become sym-

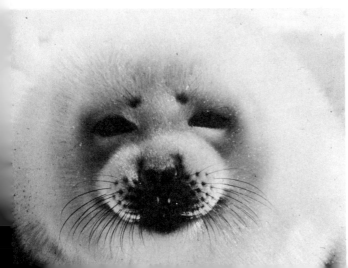

Two baby seals. These trusting wide-eyed animals are amongst the most appealing of all wildlife at such an early age. They are also helpless and totally dependent on the close attention of their mothers.

Top left. At the approach of danger the seals can slip into open water. Here they keep an eye on the author. *Top right*. Feeding a seal pup is a difficult and messy job but tremendously satisfying for all concerned. *Bottom*. Three more studies of the baby seals.

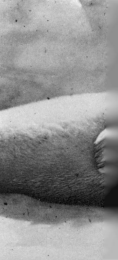

Top. The slightly apprehensive mother seal harp watches the photographer while her baby suckles peacefully. *Bottom.* The hooded seal, male and female, will defend their young to the death. When the hunters attack a family unit it means death for all three. Here the female makes her defiance known.

bolic of the torment of the other seals in the Gulf of St. Lawrence, and *did* attract a great deal of attention to the plight of these much-abused animals.

But, most important, although their life was not long, it was as long as we could make it, and I believe that for seals, as for us, life is sweet.

CHAPTER FIVE

Of Seals and Men

M Y visit to the ice floes, and later sharing my home with Jack and Jill had been fascinating and deeply moving experiences. I wanted to know more about these animals and the men who hunted them.

The origin of the harp seal is wrapped in mystery, and I could only build a shadowy background. In its modern form this species has probably not changed greatly in the past million years. Beyond that, it may descend from an otter-like creature that existed on earth some forty million years ago. And deeper in time? Who knows. Perhaps some land dwelling animal faced with changing conditions retreated back to the sea.

Born at the end of February or beginning of March, the harp seal starts life as a fluffy, yellow-white little creature weighing about fifteen pounds. Its nursery is a bare patch of sea ice some distance from the extremities of the pack ice in the Gulf of St. Lawrence.[1] Although it does not usually have a brother or sister it is surrounded by others of its kind as the females, gregarious by nature, crowd together at breeding time.

The females carry a milk that is very rich, and a baby harp seal gains weight at an extraordinary rate—some

[1] Other harp seal herds are located in the "White Sea", the "West Ice", and the "Front".

three pounds a day. On one occasion, I watched a female haul herself out of an air hole and look across at a group of pups. Seeing her, they all cried pitifully. She "humped" her way across the ice and touched noses with several before accepting one. Each of the rejected pups seemed quite prepared to claim her as mother, but she had a decided preference for only one, presumably her own baby, which she finally recognized by scent. Rolling over on her side the female "unfolded" a teat from the area of her stomach, which the young one eagerly seized. There was an almost human look of bliss on the faces of both animals as she appeared to "pump" milk into the baby. If, in fact, there is a pumping action involved it would explain the refusal on the part of Jack and Jill to suck.

Along with the weight gain comes changes in coat color. After two or three days the yellow tint fades, and the baby seal is snowy white and remains that color for a further twenty days, or so. At approximately three weeks, the white coat is shed and the animal becomes a "beater". Still a baby seal, it is grey-blue in color with scattered dark spots on its short, velvety coat. It is ready to leave the ice for the sea. The advantage of the "beater" coat at this point is obvious. It provides good camouflage in the water and protects the young seal from its great enemy, the killer whale.

For her part, the female leaves the pup when it is about $2\frac{1}{2}$ weeks old and covered in thick layers of blubber. This fat protects the young seal from cold, and provides a food supply until the animal learns to fend for itself. At first, the newly independent pup feeds on small crustaceans, but soon includes small fish in its diet.

After leaving the young, the females join the males on the ice and mate. The fertilized egg does not start to grow for about three months, and there is then a gestation period of approximately eight months. The harp seals do not pair for life, and one male may mate with several successive females. Most females bear their first pup at six or seven

51

years of age, and it is believed they may continue to bear young for a further thirteen years, or so.

In April, the immature seals and adults (but not the "beaters") gather on the ice to moult. By June, the moult has been completed and the seals have left the Gulf, and are heading north for the Davis Strait and Baffin Bay areas, a cold body of water between Canada and Greenland. There, free of their involvement with man, the seals find peace during the brief Arctic summer.

Approaching winter drives the seals south again, through the Belle Isle Strait and into the Gulf of St. Lawrence, and the cycle is complete. In early February, the pregnant females are seeking ice floes on which to have their young. But the Gulf is a huge area, roughly the size of England and Wales combined, and the ice floes do not always appear in the same place. How do the seals find the ice?

In December, as the frigid grip of winter tightens, the relatively shallow, fresh water rivers and lakes of east coast Canada usually freeze. During this period the surface of the larger body of salt water in the Gulf is chilled and sinks, to be replaced by warmer water from the depths. This process continues until the surface temperature dips below 29 degrees F., at which time ice forms. Exactly where this happens depends on local weather conditions, which vary from area to area in the Gulf, and on the ocean currents. Do the seals swim thousands of miles in a random search for ice? I rather doubt it. I believe they have developed the ability to detect minute differences in water temperatures, and that this "sense" directs them to the coldest areas of the Gulf, and ice.

I have seen ice floes up to four feet in thickness with numerous air holes scattered about. Obviously, the seals must have located the coldest area of the Gulf before ice formed. As the waters froze the seals would have broken holes, which they maintained through constant use as the surrounding ice thickened.

52

The feeding habits of the harp seals in the Gulf have been misrepresented by various politicians determined to maintain the sealing industry. They have charged that if the hunt were abolished commercial fishing would be destroyed. No responsible biologist I have spoken to agrees with this ludicrous claim. The best scientific evidence available suggests that the seals feed heavily on capelin, a non-commercial fish, when they are in the northern part of the Gulf. In the southern part of that huge inland sea where they breed, mate and moult, they eat little or nothing. In their summer waters their diet also consists mainly of non-commercial fish. The truth of the matter is that the harp seal presents no significant challenge to fishermen.

THE SEALING INDUSTRY

Although sealing vessels from Canada (mainly Newfoundland) have hunted the seals for some two hundred years, their main effort was always on the Front, where the largest herd was located. The Gulf seals were taken by occasional vessels, and a few landsmen. Just prior to the Second World War, Norway developed an interest in the seals off the east coast of Canada. Norwegian ships surveyed the potential of the Gulf herd, and the owners decided there was money to be made killing these animals. But Germany attacked, and Norway was busy for a few years. Ironically, with peace came a renewed interest in the Gulf seals, and a Norwegian company registered a few vessels in Canada. Gathering together a number of poor Canadians, and flying the Canadian flag, these vessels went after the seals.

The seals were there and the good news spread. Soon other vessels from Canada and Norway joined the hunt, and a new development in the early sixties saw ski-equipped, light aircraft and helicopters taking hunters from land to the herd. The Norwegians' main competition

53

came from the Newfoundland vessels and the aircraft. Recent developments have been the elimination of Norwegian registered vessels from the Gulf hunt, a marked drop in the number of Newfoundland vessels participating, and the banning of aircraft. This virtually leaves the field to the Norwegian company registered in Canada.

In an average year the gross value of the raw pelts taken in the Gulf would be approximately one million dollars. The net profit would be shared between the industry, the commercial hunters, and landsmen. On October 15th, 1969, the Hon. Jack Davis, Minister of Fisheries and Forestry issued a press release, which contained the following statement:

> "... Average annual returns to landsmen have been as low as $39 and as high as $102 in the past few years. The validity of these figures is open to question as the great majority of the landsmen take only three or four seals, in many cases for food. The hunters from the large vessels, however, do much better. Their average earnings, for example, were $750 in 1966, and $1,200 in 1967 for four to six weeks of work.
> ... Seven to ten large Canadian vessels are used in sealing, employing between 300 and 400 men. These vessels take the greater proportion of the seal catch. . . ."

Now we are getting to the truth!

What is the sealing industry really worth to the fishermen of eastern Canada? Let us discount the landsmen, because clearly the hunt is of very minor importance to them. The two groups that make the most money are the industry and the three or four hundred commercial hunters.

The Minister's statement that commercial hunters made from $750 to $1,200 is somewhat misleading. This figure includes their earnings for hunting at the Front (in international waters and outside the Gulf). Because of a complicated arrangement the hunters earn little if anything until enough seals have been killed to pay the owner for the operation of his vessel. This makes it difficult for me to divide exactly their total earnings in terms of Gulf and Front seals. It is, however, probably reasonable to split the figure evenly as the Canadian take of seals in the two areas is usually similar. This sees the hunter with an average annual gross income of $462·50 for hunting in the Gulf in 1966 and 1967. After paying for a berth and stoppages for income tax, etc., this becomes a figure close to the $300 many sealers have told me they earn in the Gulf. I remember one old sealer telling me that on one occasion the ship he was on did not take enough seals to pay the owners for the operation of the vessel. Not only did he suffer brutal hardship for six weeks, but on his return home he was billed for six weeks' board while on the vessel. He didn't pay it.

There is a great deal of unemployment with consequent poverty along the east coast of Canada, and average earnings in that area are low. The seal hunt only provides a total of six weeks' employment (Gulf and Front) so it is clear that most commercial seal hunters are casually employed, or unemployed during the winter. I have talked with many of them and they have told me Gulf hunt income would represent ten to twenty percent of their gross annual earnings. If the seal hunt were abolished in the Gulf it should not result in a commensurate drop in income for the men involved. Any man who will endure weeks of cruelly hard work is a worker—he could have been sitting around drawing unemployment insurance or welfare payments. With a shortened sealing sesason he would be looking for, and in many cases finding, alternative employment. And this is where the Canadian Government could help. Some of the hundreds of thousands of dollars Canada is presently spending on policing the hunt, research on harp seals, and combating an "international black eye" could be diverted to these men. Let me remind readers of what the

55

Hon. Jack Davis said to the Standing Committee on Fisheries and Forestry on March 18th, 1969. He said, in part:

> "... I looked at the administrative budget of the Department of External Affairs for this current year and it is about 50 million. I would think it would take quite a few million dollars to offset the adverse publicity[1] which Mr. Brian Davies has given Canada as a result of his recent activities, not only in New York, but abroad ..."

If the commercial Gulf hunt were stopped and Canada directly subsidized the men involved, the total annual cost would only be $185,000 ($462·50 × 400). Quite a bargain.

Of course, a handout is not the answer. Subsidised employment is. Surely, the solution to this relatively simple economic problem is not beyond the wit of the Canadian Government. Why not, for instance, create a sanctuary for the seals in the Gulf, and hire some men as wardens while the seals are in the area? They could prevent poaching, and could be utilized as guides if tourism to the area developed into a reality. And there are other areas in the Maritimes where the energies of four hundred hard working men could be put to good use for a few weeks. All that is needed is imagination, dollars, and the will. So far, the Canadian Government, angry at those who protest against the hunt, has just sulked, and made no apparent effort to seriously consider alternatives.

What about the ship owners? Subtract the hunters' earnings of $185,000 from the gross take of one million dollars and we have a high figure of $815,000. I don't know what it costs to operate "seven to ten large vessels" for two or three weeks, but I am confident, business morality in the Maritimes being what it is, that the real profits are made by the industry not the hunters. Beyond that, of course,

---

[1] The seal hunt resulted in adverse publicity for Canada, not Brian Davies. B.D.

greater profits are made by the European fur industry down to the retail level. What would these vessels do if the hunt in the Gulf were abolished? They could fish, carry cargo, or whatever they normally do during the major part of the year. The owner's profits would be lower, but I venture to suggest that is of less importance than the seals, and Canada's international reputation.

I'll let the seal hunters have the last word. Time and time again they have told me, "If there was something else I could do at this time of year I wouldn't kill seals."

CHAPTER SIX

Abolish the brutal Seal Hunt

AFTER Jack and Jill, the directors of the New Brunswick SPCA and I took stock of the situation. There was work to be done for seals that required a great deal of research if reasonable objectives were to be set and then a carefully planned program vigorously pursued. If we were to do a real job, not just wring our hands on the periphery of the problem, the "Save the Seals" Fund would have to be expanded. I would have to leave college and, as I had before, work for the New Brunswick SPCA on a full-time basis. My working time would be split between animal welfare in New Brunswick and the seals. We decided to hold a meeting of the directors at the lovely old home of Mr. and Mrs. Melvin Moore, in Gagetown, New Brunswick. At that time we would establish a policy and create the outline of a program.

I love Canada, especially in the fall and I hope my readers will excuse a brief diversion from seals.

I remember with real pleasure the one and a half hour drive along the banks of the St. John River. It was late in the year 1965, and Canada wore her fall colors with real style. The narrow road from Fredericton to Gagetown twisted and turned, climbed and dipped in obedience to the cut and thrust of the river as in years gone by it had

58

shouldered aside the rocks and soil on its journey to the sea.

Open fields with the stubble of grain crops in serried ranks drifted by my car. Suddenly, the woods would rush down to the road, and for a mile or two I would cut through the tangle of evergreens, maples, and birches that cover so much of New Brunswick. On a sudden rise, with the St. John River Valley spread below me, I'd catch a glimpse of the colorful tapestry of fall: the dark, rich greens of the spruce and pine, the crimson red of the maple, and vivid yellow of the slender birch trees. Here and there were small white farmhouses with the smoke of wood fires hanging heavy in the crystal-clear air. The bright red of apples hanging heavy on the trees appeared on my left, and I stopped the hum of the car. Walking through the undergrowth towards the trees I pushed through a myriad shades of color that no human artist could match on canvas. Reaching up, I pulled an apple from the tree and, leaning against the gnarled old trunk, enjoyed the cold crisp taste. In what I call my "fall mood", I drove on to Gagetown.

Sweeping down through the village of century-old frame houses and attractive gardens was a delightful experience. I retreated to a more spacious and leisurely age. Gathered together in the comfortable living room of the Moore Home, the directors were surrounded by antique furniture and knick-knacks. The drive from Fredericton and the charm and grace of our surroundings seemed to have combined to create a mood that would help all of us look to deeper values when considering the exploitation of animals than might normally be the case.

I looked around at the group. Melvin Moore, teacher, scholar, and administrator, volatile and clever. His wife, Frances, elegant and articulate. Alwyn Cameron, an engineer with an even temper and a keen insight into human behavior. Toby Graham, a university professor

59

possessed of keen logic. Bill Cragg, another university professor, young, enthusiastic and a loyal volunteer worker in
animal welfare. Murray Kinloch, another professor, the
Scotsman who had figured in Chapter Two. All in all,
a group limited neither in experience nor sense.

We discussed the issue for a while. I described how I
believed the hunt was carried on. We considered the survival of the species, and I passed on some of the less than
pleasant stories I had heard from people involved, at some
time or other, in the killing.

One story in particular, from a helicopter pilot resident
in Quebec, aroused the anger of the group. This pilot, in
a telephone conversation, had described to me a scene he
had witnessed off Magdalen Islands.

He said, "I saw a mother seal defending her pup. The
hunter blinded her with a blow from his club, jumped on
her back and rode her like a bucking bronco."

Finally, the chairman voiced what turned out to be our
common view. In calm measured tones he tore the hunt to
pieces.

It is wrong to destroy these animals merely to provide
inconsequential pieces of fur-trim for high-fashion clothes,
seemed to be the essence of his opening remarks. He
went on at length to explain his own personal philosophy concerning man's use of animals and to suggest that
there could be only one position for us to take: a stand for
the abolition of the brutal seal hunt in the Gulf of St.
Lawrence.

We all sat in silence for a little while, each one of us
considering the import of such a policy. When the talking
resumed, it was immediately clear that all those present
were in favor of such a stand. But I had reservations. Nothing else in this world would have given me more pleasure
than to see the seals left in peace. But I was a relative new-
comer to animal welfare work. I had not, as yet, articulated
for myself a philosophy. I tended to flounder, for instance,

when asked why we should bother with animals when human needs were so great and pressing.[1] How on earth was I going to convince anyone that it was wrong to kill seals?

I spoke up, "Frankly, I don't believe I'm intellectually capable of carrying the argument for the seals." I went on, "As the New Brunswick SPCA's only Man-Friday, the task of convincing people will fall on me. I can't do it."

"You do your best," I was told.

A small group of little people had made a big decision, a decision that would see the seal hunt become a stench in the nostrils of a large part of the world and cause the Canadian Government acute embarrassment.

[1] I now understand it is not an "either, or" situation. There is room and need for kindness to humans and animals. Indeed, how can any culture seriously interested in human welfare ignore the suffering of animals.

CHAPTER SEVEN

Weekend Magazine *and* Others

SHORTLY after the Gagetown meeting I represented the New Brunswick SPCA at the annual meeting of the Canadian Federation of Humane Societies held in Montreal. Two important events took place. I found my way to *Weekend Magazine*, and I had a long talk with two ladies, Miss H. M. Copp of Vancouver, British Columbia, and Mrs. Marjorie Wright of North Bay, Ontario.

But first, *Weekend Magazine.*

In the cold light of day, following the Gagetown meeting, I examined the various avenues open to us in pursuit of a policy that would seek to end a tradition cherished in such a place as Newfoundland, a policy that would cause the sealing industry and the European fur trade considerable difficulties.

It seemed to me at the time, and I believe events proved me right, that we should attack on three fronts. We must create in Canada a public attitude that was hostile to continued seal hunting, we must encourage a reluctance to buy harp seal pelts in Europe, and we must solicit foreign support for those Canadians wanting to end the annual massacre. A neat package-deal that I *hoped* would see the Canadian Government ban the hunt because of adverse public opinion.

A grand strategy, but where did one start? After ship-

62

ping Jack and Jill to Vancouver, the New Brunswick SPCA "Save the Seals" Fund had precisely £88.37 in the bank. Not much of a sum to bankroll an international campaign of the magnitude I envisaged. The first attack must be in Canada, and I considered the means of reaching the public available to me. They were radio, television, magazines, newspapers, and lectures. All of them could be used, but we needed, desperately, *a big break*. The more I considered the problem the more I became convinced that a magazine story with colored pictures was the answer.

Daily newspapers in Canada are a special problem to anyone needing national coverage for his pet project. Due to our vast size and other complex economic problems, newspapers have only relatively local distribution. With editorial policy varying from paper to paper, the chance of really massive support for our cause from the dailys was small.

To reach 20 million Canadians through a series of lectures would take much too long—possibly several generations of seal defenders.

It had to be a magazine story written by me and exposing the hunt. One printed publication in Canada claimed to have national coverage: *Weekend Magazine*, with headquarters in Montreal. I could attend the annual meeting of the Federation and approach the editor of *Weekend Magazine* all for the same airplane ticket.

The annual meeting was the same as all annual meetings in the animal welfare movement. For the most part, delightful people, struggling with a gigantic task.

During an afternoon session I ducked out and attempted to reach *Weekend Magazine* by bus—a frustrating means of transportation in a strange city.

With a collection of colored slides and black and white pictures in my hand, I approached the attractive young receptionist:

"I would like to talk to someone about a story on seals."

63

"Yes, sir, would you take the elevator to the sixth floor, please."

My God, I thought, it's as easy as that. I had expected to proceed no further than the front door.

Surrounded by marble and wood I found my way to the automatic elevator and was whisked to the editorial offices of *Weekend Magazine.*

Another receptionist. Again, my story.

"I'll see what I can do, sir. Please take a seat."

I picked up a back-copy of the house publication and idly leafed through it. Professional reading stories with superb photographs. My heart sank, and my earlier confidence oozed away. I was out of my league, I thought. I had nothing to offer these people. I remembered the Gagetown meeting—I was right. I wasn't equipped to play in this ball game.

Again the receptionist.

"The photo-editor, Mr. Louis Jacques, will see you, Mr. Davies."

The glass doors opened and closed on me. Desks, people, long hair, short hair, big noses, small noses, slim and fat, paper and, surprisingly, a calm quietness. For the most part, the staff of *Weekend Magazine* seemed young and were busy writing or reading.

Louis Jacques met me at the door of his modest office and gave me a warm handshake. In no time at all he had me at my ease and I was pouring out my story. Seals, seals, seals. I showed him my photographs. Using a special glass table he lit up each one in turn.

"Some are good," he said. "Leave all the material with me, and I'll see what I can do."

"Shall I call you tomorrow?"

"O.K., why don't you do that? I should have an answer by then."

And so, back to the annual meeting of the Federation.

I had long since decided, in my mind, who was the

natural leader of the Canadian Humane Movement. Miss Haroldine M. Copp, a lady of independent means, probably in her sixties, and a resident of Vancouver, British Columbia, had, for me, all the right answers. Miss Copp was superb in the rough-and-tumble of a meeting. She was logical and her transparent honesty was really refreshing. Other people's hesitations mattered little to her. What she cared about was getting the job done.

Somehow or other, I forget just how, I found myself alone with Miss Copp and her friend, Mrs. Wright, and I was telling them what we hoped to do for the seals.

Much of it was old stuff to them. They had followed the adventures of Jack and Jill and were well aware of the cruelty inherent in the hunt itself. It was when I reached the nub of the problem that their interest quickened. I explained that I must observe the real hunt—the hunt that took place when no Government inspectors were around. The hunt that saw seals subjected to unimaginable atrocities, and the hunters brutalized.

I could not reach these dark areas as a passenger in the Government helicopter. This machine was a clear danger-signal to careless or cruel hunters. To do a job, I must have my own transportation—a fixed-wing aircraft, or helicopter similar to those used by the airborne hunters. Renting machines of this type costs real money, and we had $88.37 in the bank. What I hoped for materialized: Miss Copp and Mrs. Wright immediately offered financial support.

Miss Copp pledged $1000.00 of her own money towards the cost of renting an aircraft, and asked that her donation be kept in confidence. I agreed to her request; but years later, a Committee of Canadian Members of Parliament, using the power of the Canadian House of Commons as a lever, forced me to reveal the details of Miss Copp's donation. In this circumstance, it seems to me reasonable to include in this book, with gratitude, the details that I have.

Mrs. Wright pledged $500.00 on behalf of the North Bay and District SPCA—a sum to be raised primarily by children.

We were on our way.

Strange, in retrospect, to realize that a simple meeting of friends, with a happy ending would later see me and two companions fly for long hours over the frigid waters of the Gulf, with death as a close companion.

It was time to call Louis Jacques of *Weekend Magazine,* and I was apprehensive again. I remembered, only too well, the professionalism of the publication. What on earth would they want with my few pictures and halting words? Unable to put it off any longer, I reached for the phone.

Sharply disappointed, I heard Louis say he had shown my material to the editors, and they had decided against the story. *Weekend Magazine* had done a similar item years ago with poor response. Had I not already virtually convinced myself that my story would be turned down, I would have been even more disappointed.

Here was a grinding halt before we even started. All the reasons for picking *Weekend Magazine* as our jumping-off point were still valid. Radio, T.V., and the rest still would not do the job as well. What now?

I lay on my bed struggling with the problem for about an hour; then I quit. *Weekend Magazine* it had to be, and somehow I would approach them again ...In the meantime, racking my brains was just giving me a headache.

Back in Fredericton after the Federation meeting, the directors of the "Seals" Fund and I decided to rent a light fixed-wing aircraft in order to observe the hunt independent of the Government helicopter. We could find no suitable aircraft at home and were forced to look farther afield. I travelled to Montreal again.

After some searching I heard that at a remote little airstrip in the heart of rural Quebec, there was an aircraft that might be suitable. Through a succession of bus rides and taxi trips from Montreal, I reached Saint-Jérôme. Aircraft dotted a runway ploughed out of the surrounding snow. And off in one corner stood my potential transportation to the seal hunt.

I cooled my heels in the small airport building and bought a hot-dog and coffee at the tiny restaurant. I looked through the windows at the looming forest and marvelled that anyone could make a profit in the aircraft business in such a place. Finally, Huguette Ste-Marie who, with her brother, a pilot, ran St.-Jérôme Air Service, Inc., walked with me over to the *Champion Challenger*.

A virtually new machine, it was resplendent in red and white paint. The single engine was protected from the driving snow by canvas covers. I looked at its general lines. Lots of lift with those wings, I thought, and a good power-to-weight ratio. Skis, in first-class condition, took the place of wheels. I moved closer and looked inside. A red leatherette seat for the pilot and, to his rear, a largish seat that that could accommodate, with something of a squeeze, two adults. My gaze switched to the instrument panel. Not much there: only a very rudimentary system and, damn, no radio. I had already decided that I must have a radio on the airplane we used to observe the hunt. I could imagine getting into trouble and shouting into the wind in place of a radio—a procedure that would provide precious little help.

During the discussion that followed, I was able to reach an agreement with Miss Ste-Marie that saw us rent the *Champion* for use at the seal hunt and, for extra money, a radio would be installed. We would provide our own pilot, and Ste-Jérôme Air Service, Inc. would insure delivery of the aircraft to Fredericton.

A fair day's work.

Without returning home to Fredericton, I swung north to Ottawa for a meeting with officials of the Department of Fisheries. I was going to have two strings to my bow. I would plan to have my own transportation, but would reserve two places on the Government helicopter in case something happened to the *Challenger* (and did something happen to the *Challenger!*).

Before speaking to the Fisheries people I met with Liz and Peter Simpson who had moved from Fredericton to Ottawa. Liz, bless her, agreed to act as our consultant veterinarian at the coming 1966 seal hunt, and to prepare a report. Peter would come and take photographs.

I talked with several officials of the Department of Fisheries, and I left them believing that two places on the Government helicopter were assured for the New Brunswick SPCA. Later telephone calls confirmed this arrangement. But things are seldom what they seem, and I was later to get into a terrible muddle on the Magdalen Islands.

In Ottawa, the really big break came in a chance meeting with Barbara Malone, secretary to a Member of Parliament from New Brunswick. Barbara was intensely interested in the work we had done for seals, and when she heard that I had been turned down by *Weekend Magazine* she arranged for an introduction to the magazine's Ottawa correspondent, Robert (Bob) McKeown.

I often recall that meeting in the Cafeteria of the House of Commons. Barbara, Bob and I sat down at one of the plain, plastic-topped tables, and I told the seal story once again. Bob must have been impressed.

A few weeks later I was contacted by *Weekend Magazine* and told they would run a story to appear at about the time of the 1966 seal hunt. Later, I had the pleasure of meeting Jim Quig, a writer for the magazine, who helped me with my story. I'm sure it was Jim's professional touch that made it a success.

The *crusade for the seals* could not have got off the ground without the *Weekend Magazine* story. It turned local rumblings into a national issue. Almost 5,000 readers of the magazine wrote to me, and many of them donated to the New Brunswick SPCA "Save the Seals" Fund. Almost every writer was against the hunt, and most wanted to know how they could help to stop it. One elderly lady, not wanting any advice, vowed she would travel to Ottawa to "skin the Fisheries Minister alive".

CHAPTER EIGHT

1966: For the First Time I see the Hunt

W E had an aircraft, but lacked something rather necessary—a pilot. Most of the skilled light-aircraft pilots were busy during the spring of the year. And it's not hard to guess what they were doing. They were flying on the seal hunt.

A friend of mine, Ron Smith of Fredericton, agreed to pilot the *Champion Challenger* to the hunt. Ron had flown fighters in the Canadian Air Force (RCAF), and I knew he was a fine pilot. Late in January, we pored over maps. Ron pointed to the RCAF base as Summerside, Prince Edward Island. "This would be a real good home-base for us. Lots of 'security'." A telephone call and letter to the Executive Assistant to the Canadian Minister of National Defence saw us granted permission to use the RCAF facilities. Now we had a plane, a pilot, and a base. Our plan was to return to Summerside each night and to refuel our aircraft somewhere near the actual hunt during the day's observations.

We were still faced with the problem of locating gasoline close to where we anticipated the hunt might take place. At that time, of course, we had to assume that the killing would take place off the Magdalen Islands. Imperial Esso and Eastern Provincial Airways quickly teamed up to move a cache of gasoline to the Magdalens, and Esso

70

stood by to move gasoline to Alberton, P.E.I., if a shift in wind moved the seals away from the center of the Gulf. Knowledgeable sealers claim that every five years or so the seals appear off the eastern tip of P.E.I., near Alberton, and one must always plan for this eventuality. Actually, the 1966 hunt took place close to the Magdalen Islands.

Winter clothing was borrowed. Flares and signaling mirrors were purchased, and chocolate bars wrapped in plastic. We were ready, and then: disaster. Ron was told by his employer, the New Brunswick Electric Power Commission, that he could not, after all, arrange his time schedule so that he could fly me to the hunt. This was a complete reversal of a previous decision and left me scant hours to find a replacement. I have often wondered if the change of attitude on the part of the New Brunswick Electric Power Commission, a Government agency, did not originate from a political decision in Ottawa. Under normal circumstance, one would expect at this point that our expedition could never have left the ground. I was fortunate, however, in quickly finding a replacement pilot, Bruce Taylor, a university student who was quick to volunteer when he heard of our plight.

Bruce was of medium height, overweight by about thirty pounds, balding, and wore a perpetual grin. His favourite expression was: "a few drinks, a few laughs". Bruce is a great person and larger than life.

March 5th, 1966. Time to go. Bruce and I flew to Summerside while Liz and Peter, who had joined us in Fredericton earlier, drove their car to P.E.I. Landing at the RCAF base was eventful. Equipped with skis, our aircraft landed on the piled snow beside the cleared runways. It was like riding a roller coaster and was huge fun.

Tying our *Champion* to two garbage cans full of sand, we sauntered off to find the duty officer. Bruce was convinced that we were in danger of being murdered by agents of the sealing industry, or failing that, being eaten

71

by seals. He insisted on carrying a large rifle wherever he went. Too well-mannered to object, and rather in awe of a pair that had "official sanction", the airforce personnel, although not very happy with the rifle, did their best to ignore it. Bruce, always enthusiastic, insisted on waving it at people when making a conversational point.

MARCH 6TH—THE FIRST ATTEMPT TO REACH THE MAGDALEN ISLANDS

March 6th dawned gloomily. The weather was not good for flying, and I lay on an airforce bed in my airforce room wondering what was in store for us. Later, in the mess hall, one of the pilots told me that the Canadian Government regularly spent many thousands of dollars in search and rescue during the hunt—another of the hidden costs to Canada—and very dangerous for the pilots involved as they groped through foul weather for lost seal hunters.

Later that afternoon we went downtown to the motel where Liz and Peter were. The weather had cleared and we decided that Peter and I would attempt flying to the Magdalens and back. A test run. The actual hunt would not start until March 7th.

Again the roller-coaster ride, and we were in the air. Setting course for the Magdalens, some 100 miles away, Bruce settled back in his seat, humming a tune. Jammed together in the small double seat, Peter and I looked out at a rather grim landscape. Today was no scene of beauty. A pewter colored sky with rolling, black clouds seemed to press down on us, and the snow-covered island was a study in grey. Here and there a black-colored forested area slipped beneath our wings to disappear in the whitish haze. Occasionally, we flew over small cottages with windows lighted in the dull, dark afternoon. Within minutes we were over the Gulf, and the sea ice was muddy and stained. I looked down at small broken ice floes. Totally unsuitable

72

for landing. Quite a difference from 1965.

The frozen sea stretched on, endlessly. We flew for an hour. *Where were the Magdalens?* Pencil-slim and running north to south, they were easy to miss on our northerly heading. Bruce turned to us.

"I'll give it another five minutes, then I'll fly to the west. We should pick up the islands that way."

The five minutes ran out and we made our turn. Five, ten, fifteen minutes, and still no sign of land.

"I'll try a swing to the east," said Bruce.

The plane banked sharply as we took our new course and droned on for another half-hour. Still, no sight of land.

A quick, three-way conversation over the noise of the engine, and we decided that weather and wind, marginal for light-aircraft flying, had beaten us. It was time to return to P.E.I.

Swinging about, Bruce fiddled with his plastic computer, picked up his heading and settled back. P.E.I. stretched east to west somewhere in front of us, and on our southerly heading was impossible to miss. Or so we thought.

On we flew for perhaps an hour, and not a sight of land. We had left the ice and were over open water. We could not hope to survive a forced landing. Always uneasy in a single-engine aircraft when over water, I listened carefully to the engine. A steady beat. But I could not help thinking of all the hundreds of metal pieces that made up the motor. Failure of any one could lead to disaster—long terrifying minutes as we clawed for distance with a dead engine, then the cold water. I remember trying mentally to pull P.E.I. across our course.

With still some two hours' gasoline on board, however, we were not in serious trouble. If the incredible should happen and we could not locate P.E.I., Nova Scotia and New Brunswick lay across our route, impossible to miss.

Suddenly, to our left, something tall and slim in the distance. We flew closer and realized that we were looking at a lighthouse on the extreme western tip of P.E.I. Bruce altered course and followed the shoreline to Summerside. With light rapidly failing, we rode the roller-coaster to a stop.

Later that night we decided that wind velocity must have been greater than forecast. It had pushed us farther west than Bruce computed for, and explained our confusion in the air. Or so we mistakenly thought.

WE TRY AGAIN

Clear weather and the start of the kill. This time Liz and I would make the trip. We would locate the Magdalen Islands then fly to the seals, which I heard were about 20 to 30 miles off land. Liz and I would then leave the aircraft and set about observing. Bruce would leave us alone on the ice and return for Peter. In the light of later experience, I now know this plan was hair-raising but, green as we were then, I had no conception of the danger two inexperienced people faced alone on the ice for hours. And quite how Bruce was to find us on his return, two small specks amongst thousands of seals, I had left to fate.

On this trip we had decided to leave from a civilian airport just a few miles from the RCAF base. With five hours of gasoline on board we said goodbye to Peter and lifted into the air. I looked back and saw him check his watch.

The sky was now a brilliant blue and the snow and ice glinted, gemlike. What an experience! I looked around at Liz and grinned. A quick smile back. Bruce, a silk scarf thrown carelessly around his neck, was a Battle-of-Britain pilot. He hummed tunelessly, occasionally checking his instruments or fiddling with the radio equipment. On we flew, suspended like a giant moth in a huge inverted bowl of blue.

The small broken ice floes gave way to large solid expanses of ice. And there, in the distance, ships. We had made it, or so we thought.

The small black shapes slowly grew into steel-hulled sealing vessels. In places the ice was streaked with red. We dipped lower and saw adult seals. Here and there, but difficult to pick out because of their color, were baby seals.

To our left a small, yellow aircraft slipped underneath us heading, no doubt, for the rich harvest of cruelty and dollars. Bruce turned to us and said that we should now head for the Magdalens to establish our exact location then fly back to the seals to carry out our plan.

Banking sharply to the east we set out for what we thought to be the Magdalen Islands. On we flew but, as was the case the day before, no sight of land. Gradually the large ice floes gave way to scattered smaller chunks of ice and finally we were over open water again. Land could not be far away, and Bruce changed direction. Again, a long, lonely flight. Not only could we not find land, but we were unable to pick up the ships again. Twisting and turning on new course headings we struggled to find first land, then ships, and then even ice. But no success. We were in trouble.

With perhaps half our fuel gone, Bruce decided to head back to P.E.I. It could not be more than 150 miles away and we had a good safety margin. Again, I found myself listening to the sound of the engine and looking for the odd piece of ice that we might put down on if mechanical difficulties set in. It's difficult, in retrospect, to remember just when I realized we were in very serious trouble. I think it was when we had been in the air about four hours and twenty minutes that I realized that we had only forty minutes of fuel left, and no land was in sight. I began taking close notice of Bruce.

I saw that he was frequently speaking into his microphone and trying to pick up a reply. Constantly, his head would turn to the right and left as he checked the fuel gauges above him. I didn't want to communicate my sudden anxiety to Liz, so said nothing. Silly, really, she was a bright girl and probably minutes ahead of me in noticing Bruce's concern.

A little later, Bruce turned and said, "We should have sighted land some time ago. I'm going to climb higher to see if I can get a sighting."

The minutes of fuel remaining ticked down to thirty. I looked out of the window and saw some black, brittle ice floes. Clustered together like flakes of corn in a breakfast cereal bowl, they would never hold our aircraft in the event of a crash landing.

I'll always have the greatest respect for Liz. As the minutes passed and Bruce brought the aircraft lower in order to stretch a few more miles out of the remaining gas, she didn't complain or get upset. She just sat there, looking quietly out of the window.

I checked my watch. Ten minutes fuel left and in the distance nothing but cloud banks as the weather slowly deteriorated. I suppose that the reason no one panicked was because there simply was not enough room. Jammed tightly together in the small plastic and leatherette cabin, we couldn't get our elbows free to tear at our hair or beat our chests. There was nothing to do but wait for whatever happened.

By this time Bruce was constantly shifting his gaze from the horizon to the fuel gauges.

Suddenly, he turned and said, "I believe I see land in the distance."

Long minutes passed before I could believe it was not another cloud bank.

Bruce dropped lower and P.E.I. slipped under our wings. With our skis, and the winter snow piled high, our landing ground was anywhere.

It had hardly been one of our good days, but we were going to finish it in style. With our fuel gauges registering empty we swept into a smooth landing at Summerside Airport.

Peter rushed across to meet us as Liz tumbled out in a joyful greeting. He listened in grim silence to our story and said. "I had been timing you, and just before you landed I realized that you must have used up all your fuel. You were either at the hunt or down in the sea."

None of us cared to face the prospect that we might have been down in the sea....

Later, we discussed our situation. We were not going to have another try at flying our *Champion Challenger* to the Magdalens. Something must be seriously wrong with the machine's instruments.[1] We decided instead to catch the commercial flight later that evening, and on our arrival I would claim the seats on the Government helicopter I had so providentially reserved. All was not lost, but all was not going to be easy, either. *But, easy or not, we were going to observe the hunt tomorrow. I was determined not to let the seals down.*

An uneventful trip over the same ice. Good instruments brought us to a perfect landing at Grindstone, the largest town on the Magdalens. A taxi ride to a local hotel, and I was asking Stanley Dudka for our helicopter reservations.

Oh Brother!

I had already told Stanley that the New Brunswick SPCA "Save the Seals" Fund had decided to oppose continued hunting, and the *Weekend Magazine* article had just reached the newsstands. Stanley, I believe, felt that we had taken an unreasonable attitude, and he was in no mood to cut red tape.

But let me use Stan's own words as recorded in the Minutes of Proceedings and Evidence of the House of

---

[1] Investigation later revealed gross compass errors.

Commons Standing Committee on Fisheries and Forestry at a hearing in Ottawa on Tuesday, May 20th, 1969.

"... He phoned me up the night of the first day of the hunt—and he had Dr. Simpson with him—and he demanded that he be taken on the first trip the next morning because he had to go to New York to give a lecture on the seals. I told him that the patrol would be going on the first trip and the SPCA would be going on the second trip. He demanded, and these are his words: 'I will call Diefenbaker; I will call Pearson, I will call the Minister of Fisheries.' Well, it was half-past eleven o'clock, it was a long day, and I knew he would, so I said, 'I will take one of you out'. It was agreed that I would take him and Dr. Simpson would not come along.

"One of the other SPCA members heard my conversation so he said, 'If you take him on the first trip, I want to go too or I am going to call Diefenbaker and Pearson and the Minister'. So I phoned Mr. Davies up again and I told him he would have to call whoever he was going to call because he could not go on the first trip. Apparently he did because I got a call at 2:30 a.m. telling me to take him on the second trip. They spent very little time on the ice so that they saw very few seals killed and to the best of my knowledge they left that night or the next morning for New York to give his lecture."

Two points. First, I did not go to New York to lecture in 1966, nor did I tell Stanley that I had any intention of so doing. And second, both Liz and I saw a great many seals killed. This misrepresentation of the facts is typical ... oh, what the hell. Let it pass.

Unable to find accommodation at any hotel, we had been referred to a private house. The French-speaking family who gave us shelter were kind and helpful. They gave Liz and me rooms, and the husband moved down to the living room. That was, for him, a bad move. The only telephone in the house was located next to his temporary bed. And that night I had a lot of use for that telephone.

It was very late when Stan, having changed his mind, telephoned me to say Liz and I could not go to the hunt in the Government helicopter. I told him I believed I had a commitment from the Fisheries Department with respect to definitely being provided with transportation to the hunt. Stan was obdurate, and referred me to Mr. Ross Homans (R. E. S. Homans—Regional Director— Department of Fisheries, Halifax, Nova Scotia), a senior official of his Department, who was still at Summerside. I fought with the local long distance operator and with a sulky night attendant at a motel in Summerside before I spoke to Mr. Homans. Ross could not help.

"Stan," he said, "is the man-on-the-spot and has made his decision."

I launched into a long tale of commitments made by Fisheries Department officials, and my responsibility to a great many people who were interested in the plight of the seals. Ross was as unhelpful, at that point, as Stan. Long minutes later I hung up the phone, climbed the stairs and reported events to Liz. There were only two levers left to pull. A telephone call to the Honorable H. J. Robichaud, Minister of Fisheries, presently in Ottawa or, failing co-operation from that gentleman, a call to the Right Honorable Lester B. Pearson, Prime Minister of Canada. Hell, they could only say no!

I had real difficulty getting through to Mr. Robichaud, as I didn't have his telephone number or address.

The operator in Ottawa must have thought me mad as she struggled with my lack of information compounded by a very uncertain telephone connection. Nevertheless, as is nearly always the case in North America, she did a great job, and late that night I was talking to the Minister of Fisheries.

To say the least, it was a bruising conversation that

79

went on for about half an hour. Doggedly, I kept after him and finally he gave in. Liz and I would be provided with seats on the Government helicopter.

MARCH 8TH, AT THE KILLING GROUNDS

Across from our helicopter was a baby seal with a hunter bending over it. He was starting to skin it, and as he plunged his knife into its belly the animal twisted in apparent agony, eyes and mouth wide open.

"My God! That animal is alive," said Liz.

Slipping and sliding we moved across the ice. By the time we reached the hunter the seal was dead. Its bright red blood seeped slowly into the snow, touched already with a coating of frost.

I watched Liz carefully examine the carcass.

She looked up, "I was right."

I looked at the hunter. Uncomfortable, he stood talking to a fisheries officer. Dirty grey overalls stained black with blood covered a red flannel shirt open at the neck. His poor-quality rubber boots had twisted nails driven into the heels to afford him a sure grip on the slippery surface. A cloth cap covered his head, and in place of sunglasses to protect him from the brilliant sun, he had smudged blood around his eyes. No gloves, just the steady dipping of hands into the hot blood of the dying seals kept his fingers warm. Lying beside him on the ice was his short club with a steel hook spliced to one end, and a long rope spliced to the other. I looked around me. This brutal weapon seemed so out of place against the ships, helicopters, and fixed-wing aircraft. At that moment, I think, the sheer inconsistency of the seal hunt became so apparent to me. The primitive and the sophisticated in an unholy alliance.

The Government was supplying transportation to other SPCA observers, and when they joined us on the ice we seemed to form two groups: Liz and I, and the other animal-welfare people.

Stanley Dudka was at the scene and asked all the SPCA people to stay as one party.

I objected, and said, "I have every intention of moving quietly around on my own. Dr. Simpson wants to spot-check carcasses at her discretion."

The *official party*, as it came to be known, moved off and left Liz and me with one fisheries officer as a guide.

Men dotted the ice as far as my eyes could see. Steadily, almost with a concerted rhythm, the clubs rose and fell. The hunters, working quickly, moved out in ever widening circles from their home ships.

Overhead, aircraft hurried to and from the Magdalens. I watched one in particular. Rather a dirty yellow in color, it looked shabby and cheap. Circling far beyond the ships it gently glided down and disappeared behind the thrusting pressure ridges of ice. I turned to the fisheries officer beside me and asked how many aircraft were at the hunt? He didn't know for sure, but thought about thirty-five.

I looked around for Liz, and saw her examining the seals. Moving deliberately from carcass to carcass she had started to gather the scientific data that, when published, shocked many people and angered the Canadian Government.

THE VISIT TO THE 'THETA'

Just a few hundred yards from where we stood was a small white ship called the *Theta*. Stained with rust and blood, her decks were piled high with freshly-taken pelts. The ice was extremely slippery as high winds had cleared it of snow. We only had one pair of crampons (steel spikes for boots) between us, and were having difficulty moving around. It seemed to me that if we could board the ship it would be an excellent way to see a great deal more of

81

the hunt than otherwise would be the case.

I called across to Liz and motioned towards the ship. She caught on and together we moved towards the *Theta*. I looked around and saw that our fisheries guide was following us. As we got closer to the ship a voice, amplified mechanically, boomed across the ice at us. A thick, Norwegian accent invited us aboard. Delighted, Liz and I scrambled up the wooden ladder hanging from the ship's side.

As we reached the deck we were surrounded by a grinning crew and escorted to the captain. I forget his name, but he made us welcome and sending us down to the mess hall saw that we were given hot coffee.

I didn't stay below too long, however, and was soon on deck poking around. The *Theta* was the usual grubby coaster, and seal pelts were piled on the open deck. Towering above this deck was a huge wooden platform on which rested a helicopter used to pick up pelts "panned" (piled) on the ice.

The ship had stopped, and the captain from his vantage point in the crow's-nest, was directing the men on the ice. Broken up into numerous scattered groups of from two to five men, or so it appeared, most moved with the agility that is native to the Newfoundland sealer. I watched the clubs rising and falling and saw the flashes of crimson as the knives did their work. Bent almost double the men dragged the pelts on the end of straining ropes to the scattered collection points. Marked with the ship's pennant on a long slim pole, these collection points beckoned the busy helicopter.

I watched the work. The *Theta*'s helicopter flew to a pile of bloody pelts on the ice. With deft movements a sealer attached the rope binding the pelts together to a hook trailing underneath the hovering machine. Lunging swiftly into the sky, the pilot flew his load in quick seconds to the ship. In a superb exhibition of his craft, he held his quivering aircraft a few feet off the deck and released the skins, which fell wetly. Again, the swift lunge into the air, this time to pick a dangerous path through wires, hanging ropes, and mast. Spellbound, I watched. Although I did not like the pilot's business, I had to admire his skill.

A group of men on the deck, black with dried, spattered blood, worked with the steadily mounting pile of skins. With swift movements of their sharp knives, two men removed the front flipper from each pelt. This flipper would correspond to the arm of a human and is considered a real delicacy in Newfoundland. Only one flipper is left on the pelt by the sealer on the ice, the other being removed so that the resultant hole can be used to pass a rope through. The heavy skin can then more easily be dragged over the ice to the collecting points.

As the men with the knives finished with each skin, they threw the flipper on to a steadily growing pile on the dirty deck. Even if I had not had strong reservations against eating seal flesh, I would not have fancied consuming the bloody scraps of meat and bone I saw rolling about in the dirt. Other men were piling, one upon the other, the finished seal skins, and I realized I was watching an assembly-line operation, in a sense, as coldly efficient as the manufacture of motor cars by the Ford Motor Company.

It wasn't long before we found evidence that the ship's crew had broken the seal-protection regulations. Piled in a corner were several pelts from adult seals. With their black "harps", and much coarser hair, they were unmistakable. I was later told that the hunters were forced to kill these adult females because the seals had attacked them. Frankly, in the light of my experience since then, I find it difficult to believe this. Adult harp seals have extremely limited defence territories, and if left alone are no real danger. Obviously, the men involved had wanted to kill the babies, and when the mother seals had tried to defend their young they had been beaten to death. I did not hear of any action being taken by the Fisheries Department over this particular matter, although I did report it.

Using the loud hailer the captain called the men back to the ship. Apparently, the seals had thinned out in that area and it was time to move to richer grounds. I watched the men move, cat-like, over the ice. Leaping across open stretches of water they converged on the ship with incredible speed. Then, they were swarming over the sides.

I took a good look at them. Their ages seemed to run from seventeen to seventy. Poorly clad, considering the bitter temperatures they worked in, they nonetheless seemed to suffer no apparent discomfort. Most of them were dressed in overalls similar to the kind worn by mechanics, under which were ordinary trousers and a shirt. Here and there would be a pair of sunglasses, but most of the men relied on blood smeared around their eyes to cut down the glare, which could cause sun-blindness. Cheap rubber boots and caps that could be pulled down to protect the ears completed what was, apparently, standard uniform for seal hunters. I suppose one should call them tough, but that is a gross over-simplification of the fact. The truth of the matter is that these men have just become inured to brutal discomfort. The name of the game on the seal hunt is cold and filth. After a while, anyone surviving would become used to it.

The men crowded around Liz, amazed to see a woman at the seal hunt, especially a very attractive, young woman. Friendly and courteous, they talked to us for a long time as the ship plowed through the ice. They were simple human beings, caught in the chains of a cruel industry. An industry that cared little for them, and not at all for the seals.

Again and again, sealers told me that they did not like killing seals. That if there was something else to do in the early spring they would prefer to leave the whitecoats alone. One man put it very simply.

"They're only a few days old and haven't had a chance to enjoy life."

He had made a valid point. If seals enjoy life, and I believe they do, have we the right to take it away from them without compelling reason? I think not.

I decided to climb to the crow's-nest and talk with the captain; for no other reason, really, but that I had never climbed to a crow's-nest before and it seemed like an exciting thing to do. Up the swaying mast I went, one clumsily-clad foot after the other, gripping tightly onto the iron rungs and trying to keep my camera from bumping against the metal sides. The captain, judging by his accent, was a Norwegian and kindly permitted me to join him in the rather cramped quarters. Using binoculars he was sweeping far ahead of the ship looking for faults in the ice that would ease his passage towards the richer seal fields that he believed were ahead.

Occasionally, the ship would grind to a halt because of extraordinarily heavy ice. Then, the men would scramble over the sides with dynamite and clear a passage. The shock waves of the explosion seemed to travel through the iron plates of the ship and caused my teeth to chatter. Either that, or my borrowed clothes, which were too big for me, were letting the cold in and the heat out.

Suddenly, we spotted seals and the ship, changing direction slightly, charged through the ice scattering the floes to the right and left. I saw the ship's prow skim by helpless baby seals and watched them tumble into the broken ice that heaved and tossed in our passing. Many of them must have been crushed. Down the mast I scrambled, slipping and sliding, to take my pictures. If people wouldn't believe what I said, perhaps they would believe my pictures. Busily, I photographed our passage.

ON THE ICE AGAIN

Men had gathered about the ship's sides ready to scramble down the wooden ladders and onto the ice. Liz and I joined them, anxious to get to the heart of the hunt. We had a job to do and other aspects of the hunt to cover besides sitting on a ship. Our guide from the Fisheries Department was, presumably, down in the mess hall drinking coffee and, rather mischievously I must admit, we flew the coop without him.

We tagged on to a team of five men, and, really, they were the most delightful characters. One of them was a Nova Scotian on his first seal hunt and he didn't like it one bit. He kept saying that he'd never go on a seal hunt again. I watched him throughout the afternoon, on and off, and occasionally he would spare a particular seal. It seemed that he could read in that act of mercy, forgiveness.

The rest of the men were experienced hunters and went about their killing quickly. They were anxious to harvest as many animals as possible. The oldest man, and the leader of the group, told me he had to pay board and lodging on the ship before he started making money for the seals he killed. He was anxious to reach the point at which he started to make money for himself.

After midday, we were introduced to the sealer's version of "cruising down the river on a Sunday afternoon". When our group reached a stretch of open water too wide to jump across and too large to walk around, we would float each other across on small, broken chunks of ice. The most agile man, a small, wiry young fellow, would push a block of ice out into mid-*lead* and then, like a kangaroo, would leap from the solid floe onto the smaller block of ice and, as it started to sink under his weight, would leap from that

86

to solid ice. Uncoiling his rope, he would place one end of it on the small ice chunk and push it back to the rest of the group with his gaff, a long wooden pole with a spike on one end used for just this sort of purpose. Another would then step on the piece of ice, catch hold of the rope and be pulled across. The process was repeated until all of our little band would be on firm footing again.

During one of these trips, our friend from the Fisheries Department who had joined us started to sink as he crossed the lead. Fortunately for him, the men were able to get him to solid ice with nothing worse than a wetting, but it meant that he had to make his way back to the ship and we were on our own once again.

During the afternoon I was introduced to what is to me the most distressing part of the hunt. I watched men moving in on females brave enough to stay and defend their young. With practiced efficiency, one man would confuse and frighten the female with his swinging rope while the other, and they often worked in groups of two, would rush in, grab the baby seal by its hind flippers and drag it a distance across the ice, to despatch it with his club. Swiftly skinning the animal he would race away before the mother, collecting her scattered wits, came charging after the carcass of her baby. Again and again, I saw forlorn looking female seals keeping a silent vigil before the frozen bodies of their young.

I'll not forget one occasion watching a female lying beside her pup near an open stretch of water. I had moved ahead of the killers and was sitting on a piece of ice watching them. As they moved towards this particular seal, she became very agitated and restless. Moving around her pup in defensive little circles, she turned and looked again and again at the approaching hunters. Suddenly, she slipped into the water and I thought that, as is so often the case, she had gone for good leaving her pup on the ice. But no, her head broke water and she looked at her baby. Then, holding herself almost upright in the water, she looked at the men. With a sharp little bark she heaved herself onto the ice and went once again to her pup. The men moved closer, and her baby was next. With quick, strong movements of her front flipper, she pushed the whitecoat towards the edge of the ice; and then, suddenly, into the water they went, both diving beneath the ice out of sight. I stayed there for perhaps a half-hour waiting for them to come back, but never saw sign of baby or mother. I hoped that somewhere under the ice they had found another opening, and life.

A helicopter which had been flying a regular patrol some distance away moved across towards us. I watched it settle down on the floe we were working on. A uniformed fisheries officer leaned out and beckoned me across.

"We've been looking for you for some time; we didn't know you were on that ship and were getting concerned. Are you ready to leave with us now?" he shouted above the roar of the engine.

"No. We're getting all sorts of material here. We want to stay on the ice," I said.

Looking dubious, he shut the cabin door and the helicopter took to the air. I went across to Liz and told her what had happened and suggested we'd better get as much material as we could within the next half-hour or so as I thought they would be back, this time with an order.

We worked for perhaps another hour before one of the Government helicopters settled down beside us again, and this time we were told quite firmly that it was time to return to land. We would have liked to have continued gathering material for our reports, but it was late in the afternoon and the fisheries officials felt themselves responsible for our safety.

Saying goodbye to our friends—and although we didn't like what they were doing we still felt that they were friends—we climbed into the waiting helicopter and were whisked back to our hotel. *From brutality, within minutes, to television and tea.*

MARCH 8TH, EVENING, AND THE AFTERMATH

Peter, who never did get out to see the hunt in 1966, due to lack of helicopter space, was waiting at the house for us when we arrived. The official SPCA team included representatives from Canada and the U.S.A.; and we had been invited to attend a meeting at which some form of joint policy statement could be prepared. On the surface this appeared to be a reasonable arrangement. After my recent experiences on the ice, however, I was more than ever firmly committed to trying to end the hunt. I had an intuitive feeling that a majority of the *official party* would not support this point of view. While I could add a dissenting note to their proceedings, there would be real danger that my lone voice would be lost in the sound of the big guns. I decided to boycott the meeting and speak out on my own.

My intuition was right. The *official party* later made a joint public statement and following are the key paragraphs—

"Visits were made to the icepans in the Gulf of St. Lawrence, south of the Magdalen Islands on Monday the 7th, Tuesday the 8th and Wednesday the 9th of March, 1966. The opportunity was taken to examine the skulls of many hundreds of young seals or whitecoats. These animals had been killed by men working both from ships and aircraft. Examination of the carcasses indicated that the majority of these animals had been struck on the head by some instrument with sufficient force to crush the skull.

"In our opinion these animals would have been rendered unconscious and unable to feel any pain.

"We noted that a number of the dead animals had not suffered any damage to the skulls and we were unable to satisfactorily determine whether these animals had been rendered unconscious by any other means prior to skinning.

"We feel that serious consideration should be given to developing other methods of killing seals other than clubbing or shooting.

"It is our opinion that until a better method can be developed, a club of a proper design, and properly used, is the best and most humane method of killing seals.

"It is our considered opinion that no matter what means are used to kill seals, adequate supervision is essential. In this connection our observations indicate strongly that the seal hunting regulations can only be enforced by a force of fishery officers, sufficient in numbers, and provided with the proper equipment and means of transportation. We feel that under the conditions which exist where sealing operations are carried on, adequate supervision can only be attained by the use of helicopters, and we would recommend very strongly that enough machines be provided for the specific purpose of permitting adequate supervision and continuous patrol over the ice during the hunting operation.

"We feel that there are economical and sociological reasons for seal hunting to continue, provided that adequate regulations can be drafted and enforced to ensure that all seals are killed or rendered insensitive to pain by a humane method before skinning.

"It is recommended that the Minister of Fisheries call a conference in Ottawa almost immediately, whilst experiences of all concerned are fresh in their minds, to permit full discussion of the season just concluded, and to receive representations from all interested groups, including the Department of Fisheries, conservation and humane societies and the sealing industry."

The co-signers of that report were, I am sure, attempting to gain for the seals the best deal possible. I believed at the time, and events have proved me right, that much more could be achieved. *The public was ready to embrace*

*a crusade to end the seal hunt. All that was needed was.
leadership.*

While the *official party* were still slipping and sliding
over the ice and reaching the conclusion that "there are
economical and sociological reasons for seal hunting to
continue", whatever that meant, Liz and I hit the newspapers and television, and a raging controversy erupted.
Liz said that 95% of the pup skulls she examined where
the hunters were being observed had been crushed and the
brain damage was irreparable. "But when I went a half-
mile away where they weren't being observed, I found
50% of the skulls were not crushed." She went on to tell
the reporters, "I definitely saw a baby seal being skinned
alive. It lifted its head and looked at us."

For my part (describing the events I had recently witnessed on the Gulf ice), I claimed that a ban on seal hunting was the only way to stop cruelty.

Spurred by the *Weekend Magazine* story and by what
we were now saying publicly, Canadians deluged newspaper offices with letters for publication in "Letters to
the Editor" columns. Reacting to an obvious public interest in the subject, all facets of the news media devoted a
great deal of attention to the seal hunt.

At the end of the year, I looked over my press cuttings.
I remember thinking that if what I was reading was any
measure of public opinion in my country, Canadians were
overwhelmingly opposed to the hunt. They described the
killing as savage, sadistic, tortuous and inhumane. Very
few writers or reporters rushed to the defence of the hunt
and, for the most part, those that did merely fell into the
usual pitfall of suggesting that since many other animals
were cruelly treated why bother about seals—in other
words, all they were suggesting was that one cruelty justi-
fies another.

*But Mr. Robichaud firmly resisted public pressure and
at the end of 1966, told the Canadian House of Commons*

*that he rejected demands from some quarters to abolish
the seal hunt. "Part of my duty is to protect the sealing
industry," he said.*

We had, I believe, created in Canada a public attitude
that was hostile to continued seal hunting. Now it was
time to solicit foreign support for those Canadians wanting to end the massacre. I turned to Europe.

CHAPTER NINE

The Campaign moves to Europe

SHORTLY after my return from the hunt, I received an unexpected letter from Professor, Dr. H. C. Bernhard Grzimek. This letter, and the $800 enclosed, were to lead to a close working relationship between myself and the writer. Dr. Grzimek had acquired a copy of the film taken on the 1964 seal hunt by the *Artek* people and had shown it on his television program. The response had been amazing, and thousands of Europeans, Germans in particular, had swamped Canadian embassies with hostile mail and telephone calls. He had felt it his duty to follow through. He wanted to ensure that the harp seal survived as a species in the face of the present intense hunting pressures, and he was anxious to reduce as much as possible the cruelty of the hunt. In particular, he wanted to eliminate live-skinning of baby seals. Hearing of the work we were doing, he believed he could help the seals through us.

The drive to create a sanctuary for harp seals in the Gulf of St. Lawrence would probably not have had anywhere near the success it has without the support given to us by this man.

Back to the $800. It seemed that the money had been intended to help finance observations in 1966. But these observations had already been made. The last shattered carcass lay frozen on the ice, and we were looking to

93

future goals. I had already found out, in an interview with Karl Karlsen, the Halifax ship owner who sent many vessels to the hunt, that Europe was the main market for seal-skin. I believed it was time to get our action against the use of sealskin moving in Europe and to seek European support for the mass of Canadians who wanted no part of their shabby seal hunt. I telephoned Dr. Grzimek in Frank-furt, introduced myself, and asked if I could use the money he had sent to go to Europe to meet him and generate public interest in our cause. His answer was typical:

"I gave you the money. Use it in the way you think will most benefit the seals."

I met with the directors of the New Brunswick SPCA "Save the Seals" Fund and discussed with them our next move. We all agreed that the next stop was Europe, and with Dr. Grzimek paying the bill I was to try my best.

I decided to take Joan and the children with me, so I borrowed money from my bank to pay their way. Joan was to be especially useful in an unusual meeting with a fur trader.

Dr. Grzimek wrote to tell me that he was speaking on sealing at the *Observer* Wildlife Exhibition in London, England, on April 26th. I arranged to meet him the day before his speaking engagement.

Just what else I was going to do was up to my wits.

The day we flew to England I received a telephone call from a Mr. Peter Lust of Montreal. Author of *The Last Seal Pup*, Peter was intensely interested in the seals. He told me that the *Observer*, a large British newspaper which was sponsoring the Wildlife Exhibition, had been trying to get hold of the 1964 *Artek* film but had balked at the price. A company called Mondex Films had the seal film available for rent but were asking $500·000 a show. Peter suggested that I gather together the $500·00 from some source or other, take the film to England, and hope that I could get the *Observer* or some other group to share

94

the rental cost.

"If the film has the same reaction in England as it had in Germany, it will be money well spent," said Peter.

I had a few short hours to gather the money. (One thing for sure, I didn't have it myself.) Racking my brains, I finally decided to telephone our good angel, Mrs. J. E. Hoover, of Moncton.

"Yes, it is a good cause, and I will certainly lend the money," she said.

Mrs. Hoover telephoned my bank, and I had the money. I met Peter Lust and a representative of Mondex Films at Montreal International Airport later that night and was soon on the way to England. The film *Les Phoques* was in a metal film container tucked away in our luggage.

In England, my first job was to look up a Mr. Arthur Bourne, who had worked on harp seals for the International Society for the Protection of Animals. He had, in Halifax, promised a big exposure of our cause in London, but as things turned out he was able to give little help.

I soon knew that I was on my own, and in a difficult world. In North America, one can make headway on merit. In England, one almost always has to *know* someone. My background was a Welsh mining village, and I didn't *know* anyone that had an *in* with the British *establishment*. I beat at the doors of various newspapers and tried to interest both the B.B.C. and Independent Television in the *Artek* film. But I had no luck.

I finally got a clue as to why I was having such little success. I called Colin Willock of Anglia Television, producer of the *Survival* series. He told me that pressure had been put on people higher up than himself and that he was not interested in the film *Les Phoques*. I made notes of that conversation, and still have them, so I believe that I have quoted Colin accurately.

Another clue, and this one much more direct, came from Michael Glennie. I had been having trouble finding Dr. Grzimek, who had told me to reach him at the Carlton Towers Hotel. On checking there, I learned he was not expected. There was no message directing me to any other hotel. Finally, I checked with a Mr. Calthrop of the *Observer*. He told me to contact Mr. Michael Glennie who was organizing Dr. Grzimek's visit. Michael, and I'm relying on memory now, was also primarily responsible for organizing the whole Wildlife Exhibition. I finally reached him and said I had the film, *Les Phoques*, available for his use at the exhibition.

"The Canadian High Commissioner has put strong pressure on the *Observer* and the Council of Wildlife not to show *Les Phoques*. Both groups have yielded to this pressure," he replied (I have notes of this conversation).

I think it's reasonable for me to say that I now had a pretty good idea of what agency was blocking my attempt to reach the British public with the story of the Canadian seal hunt.

At this point events started going from bad to worse. I never did contact Dr. Grzimek before he gave his talk and wasn't present when he spoke at the Wildlife Exhibition. He did, however, have a film to show. This was one taken by Dr. Harry Lillie, years ago, which, so I was told, included a statement by the Canadian Government that cruelties depicted did not now occur in the modern seal hunt. *What rubbish!* But I was the only man in England at that time with the experience to say so, and no one would listen to me.

I did finally contact Dr. Grzimek by telephone and arranged to meet him on April 27th, in the lobby of the Royal Garden Hotel.

Arther Bourne joined me, and together with Dr. Grzimek we sat in the crowded public lobby of the hotel while I told my story. I'd learned enough during my few days in London to become convinced that our German friend was a key figure. With him on our side, we stood a

96

good chance of winning. This was an important meeting. Somehow or other, in spite of the multitude of people milling around, I had to transmit to Dr. Grzimek my utter conviction that the seal hunt was cruel, and that there was no way of making it not cruel. If I could convince him of that, then I could ask him to expose the real cost of sealskin products on his television program. What a tremendous kick-off for our campaign that would be! Carefully, I picked my way through the story. Dr. Grzimek sat there chain-smoking as he listened to me. He was obviously a sensitive, intense person.

As he talked to Arthur Bourne, I studied Dr. Grzimek carefully. Tall and slim, with carefully groomed grey hair, he was dressed conservatively. With nervous motions, he involved himself in our total conversation. Dr. Grzimek questioned me closely on Dr. Simpson's findings and expressed shock at the large percentage of uncrushed skulls she had found in her examination of carcasses.

I had talked myself out and was watching for his reaction. His nervousness, or perhaps shyness, had dissipated as he took my measure and grasped the subject. I saw his blue eyes take on a careful look. He sat for a few moments in silence and, carefully choosing his words, told me the position he would take.

"We must give the Canadian Government one more year to improve matters. I think it would be unreasonable to call for a boycott of baby seal pelts on my television program without having given them this extra time.

"I will, however, help finance an air-photo survey of the seal herds next year."

I broke in: "Do you agree with the principle of a sanctuary for harp seals in the Gulf of St. Lawrence?"

"Yes, I do. This would be a wonderful thing, but I think we would be aiming too high."

Disheartened, I left the meeting. Perhaps I should have stayed in Canada.

97

There were two more blows to fall.

I had been in contact with Mr. Trevor Scott, Chief Administrator of the International Society for the Protection of Animals (ISPA). He had told me that the directors of ISPA were meeting in London and that they would consider a report on the Canadian seal hunt. I was extremely anxious to have ISPA adopt a policy of abolition and asked Trevor if it would be possible for me to speak to them. He and I knew that I was the only person in England, at that time, who had actually witnessed recent events in the Gulf. It seemed only sensible for the directors of this international animal welfare society to have me available to answer questions that must obviously arise. With the total lack of imagination that seems to be so typical of some in the established humane movement, the ISPA directors refused to talk with me. At that time, Joan and I coined a phrase which, with certain modifications that depend on the company we happen to be keeping at the time, we often use. *God help animals ... no one else will.*

Back at our hotel I re-wrote the *Weekend Magazine* article in a form that brought it up to date with the 1966 hunt and would, I hoped, make it suitable for publication in a British newspaper.

In a final attempt to create some interest in the plight of the seals I went to the *People*, a very large Sunday newspaper. I left the article with the gentleman at the desk and was told I would be contacted. I would have liked to have left it with somebody a bit more important than the gentleman at the desk, but that was as far as I could get. Eventually, I was contacted and told the newspaper wasn't interested.

One afternoon Joan and I decided that we would do a bit of private research on the sealskin trade in Europe. We were outside a telephone booth in Paddington Railway Station and, to a great extent on impulse, I went inside and began searching through the phone book. Looking up fur traders, I saw MacMillan and Moore Co., Limited, and gave them a call. I spoke to Mr. MacMillan and, feeling like Sherlock Holmes in disguise, I told him I was interested in buying my wife a sealskin coat. I was told he didn't sell the finished garment but that we could look at some pelts. Would we come around now? You bet we would.

By the time we reached Mr. MacMillan, we had changed our fictitious story. I was a seal hunter who used aircraft in the Gulf and was tired of selling my pelts to Mr. Karl Karlsen who kept prices low, I claimed.

Mr. MacMillan was a tallish man of rather heavy build. Wearing a long, white coat like a butcher's, he had a rather genial air about him. His office was small, but quite tastefully furnished. We sat and talked for a while, and he revealed a lot about the sealing industry. He told me who spoke the truth and who lied, at least in his opinion, but I don't think I'll include his comments here.

The information we received from Mr. MacMillan may not have been obtained altogether ethically, but it formed the basis of more research that I might not have been directed to by any other agency. Before we left he showed us around his warehouse.

I imagine most people would have looked at the bales of fur, the one-dimensional muskrat, leopard, beaver, etc., without considering much else but the beauty of the pelts. But I had been at the sharp end of fur procurement, and I had good reason to look beyond. I tried to calculate the immense cost in agony that the piles of fur before me represented. I gave it up ... it was obviously astronomical. I came away convinced that animals pay too high a price for our luxury fur trade.

On May 11th, we returned to Canada having helped the seals little. Our best efforts had been blocked.

My charges, carried in Canadian newspapers, that the

Canadian High Commissioner in London had brought pressure on a London newspaper not to show a film depicting atrocities in the seal hunt in the Gulf of St. Lawrence were haughtily rejected in the Canadian House of Commons. And the "faked film" label began to be applied "officially" to any who sought to expose the seal hunt.

CHAPTER TEN

The "Faked" Film Smear

THE *faked film* smear would bedevil all my work for the seals, and it is time the facts, as I believe them to be, are set out.

In 1964, a Canadian Company called *Artek Films, Ltd.*, contracted with the Canadian Broadcasting Company to produce thirty-nine films on fishing and hunting in the Province of Quebec. In conjunction with this contract, but as a special project, *Artek Films* decided to make a film on seals. A crew left for the Magdalen Islands in late February of that year, knowing nothing of the hunt, and expecting to shoot film of seals in their natural habitat.

Flying from the mainland to the islands, the film crew noticed ships and light aircraft milling around the blood-stained sea ice. *The Canadian seal hunt had been discovered.* With their cameras and hard-hitting text, *Artek* would give the shabby operation a blow from which it would never recover. Later, the *Artek Film* crew, André Fleury, Serge Deyglun, Uwe Koneman, André Legault, and Gratien Roy, would find an angry Canadian Government bent on destroying their personal and professional reputations. I know André Fleury and Serge Deyglun fairly well. I have found them scrupulously honest. I do not believe that they would deliberately stage scenes of cruelty. And even if they were capable of manipulation there is no need for it on the seal hunt. Cruelty surrounds the photographer, and the trick is to get it on film before vomiting.

The scene challenged by the Canadian Government shows a hunter standing near a large seal. He is prodding at the animal with his knife. This is done two or three times, and on each occasion the seal turns and lunges at its tormentor. The film lasts some forty minutes, and the scene in question some very few seconds. The rest of the film, which shows much more horrifying sequences, is not seriously challenged by those in authority.

When the controversy about the seal hunt erupted, the Fisheries Minister, Mr. Robichaud, cried "faked film". Identifying it as the *Artek* film, in the Canadian House of Commons where he is immune from civil action, the defender of the seal hunt outside the House, just talked in broad general terms of "faked films". Consequently, those who had a film concerning the seal hunt found their property highly suspect. Anyone with a grain of sense can see the effectiveness of such tactics. But whether the end justified the means is another question. In spite of frequently having my name linked to the "faked film" on seal hunting, I saw the *Artek* film for the first time in the spring of 1969.

On December 10th, 1966, in a *Canadian Press* release carried in the *Toronto Globe and Mail*, Mr. Robichaud was quoted as saying, "The Government has obtained affidavits asserting that men who skinned a baby seal alive before a movie camera were paid to do so."

All I could find upon examining the affidavits in question was one signed declaration that read as follows:

"I, the undersigned, Gustave A. Poirier of Magdalen Islands declare having been employed by a group of photographers, one of whom had a beard, around March 3, 1964, to skin a large seal for a film. I solemnly declare before witnesses that I was asked to torment the said seal and not to use a stick, but just to use a knife to carry out this operation where in a normal practice a stick is used to first kill the seals before skinning them."

Mr. Robichaud, in commenting on this particular gem, said, "I feel this is enough evidence to prove without a doubt that the film referred to, taken in 1964, was staged for a definite purpose."

When I was watching the film for the first time in 1969, Mr. Gustave A. Poirier was identified as the gentleman prodding a large seal. While there is no doubt in my mind that baby seals of some thirty or so pounds are skinned alive, I do not for one moment believe that three to five hundred pound adult seals suffer the same fate. I do not believe that Mr. Poirier, using only a knife, could possibly have skinned alive an adult, or to use his words, "a large seal". And, surprisingly enough, I have support for my belief from a rather strange source, everything considered.

The *Victoria Daily Times* of October 27th, 1964, quotes a Fisheries Department spokesman as saying,

"This is absolute unadulterated hogwash. Can you picture a seal hunter attempting to skin alive a three-hundred pound adult seal? He'd have his hands full!"

He certainly would have his hands full. Who or what is getting skinned in this controversy? The people who made the *Artek* Film? Me? The consciences of certain members of parliament? The credulity of the public? Or all together?

Remember, the hunter was prodding at an adult seal. Somehow or other an adult seal being prodded becomes a baby seal skinned alive. Quite how the elected representatives of the Canadian people managed to cope with the mental gymnastics required and still keep their self respect is beyond me.

Paris-Match ran a sequence of still pictures of the 1969 hunt that perfectly duplicated the knife-prodding scene in the *Artek* film. I was there when the photographer for the French magazine took these particular shots, and I know there was no attempt at faking anything. The hunter in 1969 was trying to drive an adult female from the freshly-killed carcass of her pup. Six years after the *Artek* film, and in spite of all the regulations, here was virtually the same terrible scene.

CHAPTER ELEVEN

The 1967 Hunt

DR. GRZIMEK was still interested in the plight of the seals and was determined to see a *real* improvement made. He had access to funds that were far beyond anything we could develop within Canada, and when he offered to finance observation of the hunt in 1967 we jumped at his offer. He wanted more scientific data to substantiate charges of cruelty if in fact cruelty had still not been eliminated.

I lined up a helicopter and a fixed-wing light aircraft, and asked Liz and Peter if they would again join the team. Liz, now a veterinary pathologist at Cambridge University, was living in England. Peter, a geologist, agreed to accompany me as a photographer.

Early March saw our preparations completed, and this time we were in position on the Magdalen Islands in advance of the opening day of the hunt. Besides Liz and Peter Simpson and myself, the team included Dr. Arne Johansen, a veterinarian representing the Canadian SPCA (a fine organization which has consistently fought the seal hunt); Ralph Kay, a friend of mine from Fredericton—a professional photographer who would take a sequence of moving pictures which would shock everyone; Fred Beairsto, a volunteer director of the New Brunswick SPCA "Save the Seals" Fund; John Gray, a newspaper reporter from the *Montreal Star*, an influential daily newspaper; and two pilots and an engineer to fly and care for our aircraft. There were too many people for the seats we had available, but luck was to be on our side in 1967.

By now the Magdalen Islanders, who believed, erroneously in my opinion, that the hunt was important to their economy, had recognized that Brian Davies was out to stop the seal hunt. It was obvious that I was not welcome on their islands. The feeling of tension was tangible. I didn't like it, one bit. For me, the islands seemed to be smothered in a blanket of hostility.

I remember on one occasion walking to the shopping area in Grindstone, the largest town, to find a milling group of seal hunters assembled. Men of the Islands, they had gathered in the town to purchase seal hunting licenses and equipment. Clad in dark clothes with long sharp knives at their side they appeared, no doubt due to my overactive imagination, very sinister. Convinced that a thousand imaginary knives were being plunged between my shoulder blades, I hurriedly completed my business.

In retrospect, all this seems a bit emotional really. But being Brian Davies on the Magdalen Islands in the spring of the year is a rather uncomfortable experience.

RECONNAISSANCE

During the afternoon prior to opening day, I decided to fly out in the fixed-wing aircraft to reconnoitre the situation. We needed to know exactly where the seals were, prior to the start of the hunt. Once I found the herd I would be left on the ice and the aircraft would return and, together with the helicopter, would transport the rest of my party as rapidly as possible to my location. It was our intention to study and photograph the seals prior to the hunt. I felt that we could evoke more sympathy for them by showing the killing against the background of their happy family life.

We swept over the ice at about 3,000 feet in order not to disturb any of the isolated patches of seals that might be on the fringe of the main herd. The enchanting beauty of 1965 and 1966 was again everywhere. In a few short minutes we sighted a large group of animals and glided to a landing on a near-by empty ice floe.

The sequence of events that always took place prior to our aircraft's coming to rest was a lot more complicated than my previous sentence might suggest. Alex Morrison, my pilot, was an experienced ex-seal-hunting flyer (he had sickened of the hunt) and knew just the sort of ice to head for. He would fly over the chosen landing area east to west, north to south, checking it carefully at practically zero feet for any flaws that might break up our skis and then our aircraft on landing. This was a manoeuver that had to be repeated several times to ensure that there were no cracks hidden by snow. And it was great fun. Finally, with power shut down and close to stalling, Alex would allow the machine to settle, oh, so gently, on the frozen ice and snow. With quick movements of his rudder, he avoided the inevitable lumps of frozen snow in his path, and as the jagged edge of the chosen ice floe clawed towards us he would sometimes whip the machine around in a hundred and eighty degree turn and apply full power. Almost immediately, when he did this, the machine would come to a shuddering halt. Quite a manoeuver!

Gleefully, on this first occasion, I jumped out of my red plastic cockpit and felt the gentle roll of the sea ice under my feet. Alex joined me, and we strolled about the ice floe stretching our legs a little. Then Alex climbed back into the aircraft and took off for the rest of my party. We didn't plan it that way, but I wouldn't see him or the aircraft again for several hours.

Without the fussy little machine beside me, I felt somewhat lost. But over in the distance were seals. Beautiful,

107

exciting seals. Hundreds of them.

I crept towards the edge of my ice floe and moved from one broken chunk of ice to another. Carefully keeping downwind of the animals, I moved closer and closer towards them. I suppose the whole "stalk" took the best part of a half-hour, and that was my undoing.

I was flat on my stomach and crawling across an open piece of ice, very close to the seals, when there was a roar above me, and Alex and his aircraft, disappeared into the distance. Belatedly, I jumped to my feet and waved my arms. Too late. I had been missed on the first run, and now my pilot would have difficulty locating me. There wasn't anything I could do about it and I settled down to enjoy watching the seals.

This particular group of animals may have all been males as there were no babies in sight. Occasionally, one or more of the big beasts would slip off the edge of the ice into the cold blue water and, swimming swiftly, race back and forth across the open *lead*. Happy, I watched my private "show" for perhaps one and a half hours. Then it became obvious that the light was failing as evening approached.

Climbing to my feet I walked quickly back to our impromptu airfield and, sitting on a large chunk of ice, wondered what I should do. I looked up, but the sky seemed singularly empty of aircraft. At any other time the damned things would be buzzing around like mosquitoes, but when one needs one, it's never there.

I decided to kick an SOS sign in the frozen snow. Unfortunately, the snow was frozen to such an extent that I could not penetrate more than one half inch, and my SOS sign looked rather weak and lost in the hundreds of square miles of ice surrounding me. The sun was going down rapidly and it was getting very cold. I had no food or drink with me, and it seemed as though I might be faced with a long cold night on my piece of unyielding frozen water. I can remember that I wasn't frightened at the prospect of staying on the floating ice overnight, but that I wasn't looking forward to the boredom of it all either. Once it became dark there would be no seals to look at and no hope of being found. I would be left, quite literally, cooling my heels in the middle of the Gulf of St. Lawrence. Not a very attractive proposition!

I had in my pocket a couple of flares I had bought at a local automotive store, which were for the use of motorists who have flat tires and what-have-you on the road. I was rather proud of my foresight, and busily practiced in my mind how I would light one of these flares and wave it professionally at any aircraft that might fly by.

The afternoon wore on and I gave up hope of rescue. In fact, I had begun to think of what might happen if a storm blew up. Then, the ice floes buckle and heave, and it is a good idea not to be standing on a piece of ice that develops a crack. If I was, and if slow to move, I would suddenly find myself doing the "splits" over open water with one piece of my ice floe drifting off to the right and the other to the left. This state of affairs would last for perhaps a fraction of a second before I was up to my neck in the freezing waters of the Gulf, with short moments to live.

Suddenly, a small dot appeared in the distance travelling low and quickly across the ice. I watched it carefully. It came closer and closer. I pulled out one of my flares and set light to it. There I stood like a miniature Statue of Liberty while what was obviously my helicopter clattered towards me. Within seconds I was in the air and heading back to land.

"So you saw my flare," I said to my pilot.

His answer rather deflated me: "No, we just saw you standing on the ice."

My esteemed flare had been practically invisible to anyone except myself.

It was dark by the time we reached the small airport on the Magdalen Islands where I was given a warm welcome by Peter, Fred, and Ralph. Liz was out with Alex Morrison, still looking for me. The sun had disappeared completely, and the evening was black and cold when Alex finally landed. His relief at finding me safe and sound was almost comical. Apparently, he had searched the ice floes for hours and in final desperation had sent out a "mayday" call which had been answered by Rescue Headquarters in Halifax.

I went quickly to the telephone in the terminal of the small airport and called Rescue Headquarters to tell them that there was no need to send a helicopter equipped with lights to search for me. The gentleman on the other end of the line was quite kind and made the helpful suggestion that next time I go out I tie a long piece of colored ribbon to my toe so that people could find me.

I learned later, that Alex had jokingly been offered money by sealers to lose me on the ice, and was terrified that I might suspect him of deliberately abandoning me that night. Of course, I didn't.

THE HUNT OPENS

Early on opening day I drove our rented truck to the airstrip. It was bitterly cold.

I looked out at a cluster of fifteen or so aircraft: one helicopter, the rest fixed-wing. They turned the little frozen bay into a miniature airfield. I sensed trouble. With the exception of our two aircraft, they were all operated by seal hunters. Their pilots would be pushing up to and eventually beyond all safety limits. There would be no control. All we could do was keep our fingers crossed and hope that we would not be involved in any mid-air collisions.

I watched Alex pull the canvas cover from his engine

and gas-up. I looked gloomily at our bright red gasoline drums. With SPCA chalked on them they were a sitting invitation to trouble. I wondered if some kind soul had put sugar in them. We would soon find out.

I heard an engine revving hard from an adjacent strip. I couldn't see the aircraft make its run down the frozen snow, but the snarling roar was as good as sight. The engine sounded louder and louder and then, suddenly, silence. No softening murmur as the pilot throttled back and headed out to the seals. Someone had crashed.

I remember thinking, as I climbed into Alex's aircraft, that saving seals does have its drawbacks.

I had decided to again reconnoitre the seal herd to find the best drop-point for our party.

As in 1966, our most important task was the gathering of evidence on the effectiveness or otherwise of killing methods. This would come from autopsies carried out by the two vets. The Fisheries Department, personified by Mr. Robichaud, had strongly challenged the evidence which we had gathered in 1966. "It's impossible to skin a baby seal alive. Why, the hunter would cut his fingers" seemed to be the essence of the defence of the hunt. No one has explained to me why, if this is the case, the Seal-Protection Regulations contained, and still do, a section that prohibits the skinning alive of seals.

It was in 1966 that I had noticed a strange phenomena. About half of the baby seals I observed would tuck in their heads, puff themselves up like little white balls, and freeze at the approach of man. Similar reactions can be found in several species, notably the opossum. I believed that in this "play dead" condition, with the skull covered by a thick layer of fat, the seal would be difficult to kill by a blow on the head. The hunter, having administered a blow, would assume that the animal was soundly unconscious or dead and go about his business. The unfortunate seal, if it could suffer pain in this state of suspended

111

animation, would be out of luck. Within seconds the skin would be ripped from its living body and the busy hunter would have moved on. I believe that much of the evidence we have found of uncrushed skulls results from this "play dead" reaction of the seals and that charges that animals are skinned alive are well-founded.

I have often wondered why the seal exhibits this reaction and have formulated a theory. The harp seal is born with a yellowish-white fur or, if one wants to be technical, hair-coat. Within a very few days the yellow tinge is lost and the seal is snowy white. During this "yellow" period the mother seal is very defensive and will often defend her pup from predators. With the appearance of the white coat the female becomes less defensive and will often leave the pup when hunters approach. The "white" color of the baby seal, coupled with lack of movement, forms an effective camouflage against the snow, and the retreat of the mother makes good sense. She sticks out like a sore thumb on the ice and attracts trouble.

I can only account for the fact that perhaps half of the seals do not adopt this "play dead" attitude by suggesting that changing evolutionary patterns are at work on the harp seal. Hardly any predators in modern time, other than man, threaten the young seals in their relatively southern breeding areas. It is possible that a warmer climate has resulted in more frequent breaking of the ice pans with consequent heavier mortality from that fact. Highly mobile young seals that do not adopt the "play dead" reaction I have described when fearful would stand a better chance of escaping from the crushing effects of falling ice blocks. Perhaps, if man allows the harp seal to live with him in this crowded world, there may come a day when the "play dead" reaction of the baby seal will have disappeared.

I looked out at the heavy ice that covered the Gulf that year. Within minutes, or so it seemed, we had sighted the

Top. A mother seal harp and her new-born pup. *Bottom.* The seals cluster round the *leads.* In any given year about a million of these animals migrate to the gulf and could make a major tourist attraction.

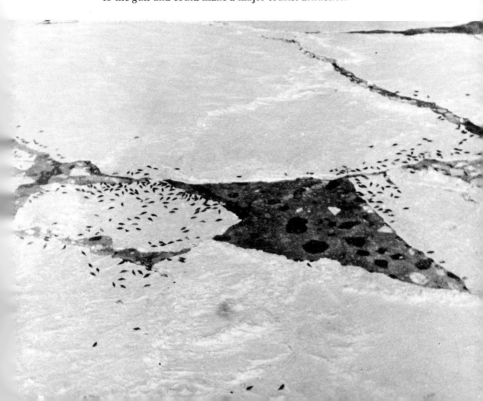

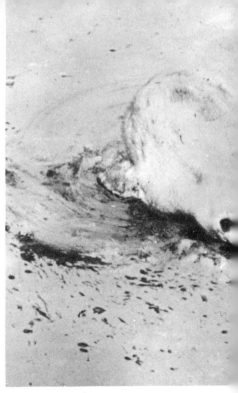

Top left and bottom. A macabre procession from the first blow with a club to the flag marked pile of blood stained pelts.

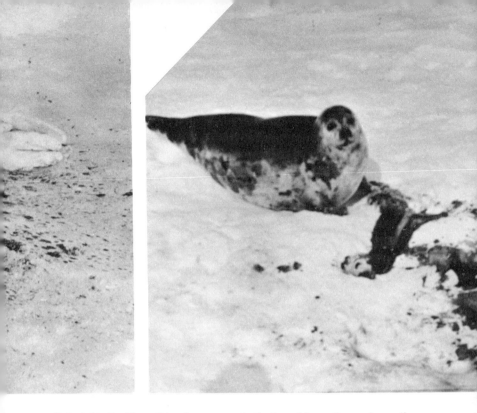

Top right. Could anything be more pathetic than this mother seal guarding the skinned carcase of her pup? *Top centre.* This pup was obviously alive when the hunter stabbed it. Its dying struggles are outlined on the snow in blood.

Top. Helicopters are used to collect the pelts into large bundles which are dropped close to the seal ships. *Bottom.* On board the Theta men busily pile the pelts and remove the flippers.

ships. Sweeping in low Alex pointed out the black snake-
like lines of hunters to me. He dipped down over a thickly
populated floe, and we saw the clubs at their brutal work
again. In a brief reconnaissance we located suitable ice,
touched down in a practice landing, and were on our way
back to the shore party. I had decided that no one was to
be left on the ice alone because of my experience the
previous night. Two people could still run into trouble,
but two on the ice stood a better chance than one.

Quickly, the first lift comprising myself, Liz and Dr.
Johansen was on the ice and at work. Liz, this being her
second year, was more a veterinary-pathologist and less a
tourist. Dr. Johansen, this being his first year, was just the
reverse. I stayed with the small dump of food and gasoline
that we established on the ice to wait for the rest of the
party. There was a touch of humour in watching my friends
as they arrived in the aircraft.

Fred Beairsto is not slim. Given to pampering himself
under the best of circumstances, he had taken extraordinary precautions to ensure that he would not be cold,
hungry, or thirsty on the ice. Loaded down with goodies,
he occupied two seats on our three-seat helicopter. When
the cabin door opened he more or less fell out onto the ice
in a jumble of topcoat, innumerable sweaters, and dozens
of scarves. Packages of sandwiches and bottles of water
bulged all over his round body. Exaggerating to an extent,
I might say that as the day progressed it became more and
more difficult to distinguish Fred from a seal.

Peter, who had been balked of a visit to the seal herd
in 1966 and who had listened to Liz and me talk at length
about the wonders of the ice floes since that time, was absolutely beside himself with excitement. He had with him
a large rucksack in the middle of which was a tape recorder.
I didn't realize this at the time and couldn't imagine why
on getting out of the aircraft he rushed across to me, put
his rucksack on the ground, and suddenly started talking

to it. The high pitched tone of his voice and his precise "radio-operator" style amused us all and was quite a tonic.

Ralph Kay was quite calm and walked quickly across to me carrying his movie camera. Ralph was to play a key role and required some very special instructions. I was sick to death of the "fake film" business and wanted to ensure that nothing similar could be charged with respect to the film that we would make this year. I told Ralph that under no circumstances was he to ask a sealer to perform any act; I told him he was not even to talk to a sealer. He was merely to follow the hunt and as fairly as he could, document what he saw through the lens of his camera.

John Gray, the newspaper reporter, was in a similar situation. I asked John for nothing and made no effort to influence his reporting. Even if I had, John was not the sort of person to be influenced by anyone. He wrote, I believe, as he saw events.

Everyone had a good day. The ice was solid and the new people had no problems. Our aircraft worked well, and I think that we observed a good cross-section of the hunt.

Fairly late in the afternoon, I decided to play safe and start moving my people back to land. Striking a heroic pose, I said that I would be the last man on the ice. Everything went very smoothly until only Ralph Kay and I remained. Then, unaccountably to us, our wait for the returning aircraft stretched out into a long time.

There were several crashed aircraft in the vicinity—1967 was a bad year for airborne seal hunters—and we moved across to the fuselage of one of them for shelter. It got colder as the sky darkened, and we were considering whether we should stay the night in the smashed aircraft or try to make our way to one of the sealing ships. I told Ralph that he could do what he liked, but I wasn't going to any sealing ship. I would stay in the aircraft. Leaning against a broken wing, we watched flights of aircraft working busily back and forth over the ice until just when we had given up hope of rescue a small green aircraft landed beside us. A cheery young face looked out.

"Your fixed-wing has crashed, and I am here to pick up one of you. Sorry, but I don't have the necessary lift to take you both. Too much weight."

It was at this point I regretted my previous, heroic posture.

"Oh, there's just no question about it Ralph, you must go. I'll stay here. No problem," I said quickly.

It sure as hell was a problem. Twice on successive nights was getting to be more than a joke. I watched Ralph take to the air and then retreated, gloomily, to my tent of twisted aluminum and fabric.

Later, with growing hope I watched two helicopters flying across the ice towards me, but they were there to retrieve shattered aircraft, not stranded SPCA observers. Forgetting my own predicament for the moment, I watched enthralled as they slung cables around one of the wrecks and lifting it high into the air start their journey back to land.

But I was going to sleep in a bed that night after all. In the distance I could see a machine with the distinctive red tanks of our helicopter. A little later I was sitting comfortably in the heated cabin and on my way back to Grindstone.

I found out that lack of control at the landing strip was largely responsible for the accident to our fixed-wing aircraft. Alex had taken off only to ram full tilt into a full, 45-gallon drum of high octane aviation gasoline. His whirling propeller had sliced the top off the drum and gasoline had spilled everywhere. Had there been a spark, Alex would have been incinerated within seconds. Luck was with us. And luck continued to be with us when after repairs the aircraft was able to fly the next day.

DAY TWO OF THE HUNT: THE WEATHER FRUSTRATES US

On the next day the whole party went out to land beside one of the ships, and we worked around that general area for a short while. Suddenly the weather deteriorated, and it was time to get back to land, and fast.

Liz and Peter elected to try to find accommodation on a passing ship in order to cut down on the number of times our aircraft had to make return trips back and forth to the land. This increased our safety margin. Excited as a pair of school kids, they reported they had been offered accommodation for the night. Scrambling aboard the same ship as it passed me on the ice, I made my way to the bridge, introduced myself, and asked for similar accommodation. Not surprisingly, I suppose, the offer of my company was declined, and I made my way back to the helicopter. With no problems, back on shore I assembled all the party and, packed into our rented truck, we drove back to the hotel.

The weather continued poor for the next thirty or forty hours, and it was some time before we retrieved Liz and Peter from their sealing friends. When we did, however, we found they had been very well treated and had had quite an experience.

THE CLOSE OF THE 1967 HUNT

There was one more good day of observing the hunt before we decided to close down our operation. The Canadian Government quota of 50,000 seals was rapidly being reached

What were the results? Had we found anything new? Had the hunt improved? Should we go on with our quest to end the slaughter?

In spite of the best efforts of the Fisheries Officers (and they had been trying hard, it must be admitted), many seals were still alive as the hunters started to skin them.

The gross brutality to intelligent young mammals was still dreadfully apparent. The destruction of beauty was no less appalling. Had we got any new weapons in our arsenal?

Liz's report would confirm our charge that the seal hunt was cruel. Ralph's film, in spite of numerous technical problems, would prove to be a shocker, and would be widely shown all over the world. And John Gray would write an article and subsequent editorials in the *Montreal Star* that strengthened and improved our support all across Canada.

Shortly after the 1967 hunt I again travelled to Europe, the centre of the sealskin trade—I was determined to make the killing of these animals an international scandal. Meeting with more success than in 1966, I was able to reach people in many countries through a series of press conferences, public meetings and radio and television interviews. It was hard work, but it was doing the job. There really was a quickening of interest, and I laid plans for the 1968 hunt.

CHAPTER TWELVE

The Pribilof Islands Fur-Seal Hunt

THE harp seal controversy focussed attention on seal hunts in other parts of the world. And in mid-1967, I represented the Swiss Aktionskomitee gegen den Robbenmord, the German Zoological Gesellschaft von 1958 (the conservation society Dr. Grzimek was associated with), the Humane Society of the United States (HSUS), and the Canadian Association for the Protection of Fur-Bearing Animals, at the "Pribilof Fur-Seal Harvest". I was concerned by this switch in emphasis away from the harp seals as I had often stressed the need for humane societies to set limited and attainable goals. Repeatedly, I had warned against the diversion of effort that saw the best intentions of those in animal welfare lead to nothing but heartbreak. Why then did I agree to go to the Pribilof Islands?

The interest in harp seals had resulted—and this is a most important point—in a growing public awareness of animals, and the problems they have in sharing the planet Earth with humans. Inevitably, attention would tend to focus on the plight of other species of seals. Some people thought the slaughter of fur seals by American civil servants was ripe for challenge. I agreed with them and judged that the fight for these seals could be concentrated in the U.S.A., and therefore should not attract interest away from the harp seal battle in Canada and Europe. In any

118

event, the fur seals had as much right to relief as did the harp seals, and it was no part of my business to suggest to anyone that they ignore the plight of other animals.

The summer of 1967 saw me flying from Fredericton to Anchorage, Alaska.

I had been told Alaska was the last American Frontier, and I was looking forward to seeing totally new ground. The flight up the West Coast from Seattle in the State of Washington was, however, hardly scenic. Thick, swirling cloud lay between my aircraft and some of the most beautiful country in the world. Never one to fret about the unattainable I contentedly read books and magazines during the long flight. Anchorage International Airport did not impress me. Poorly designed and cheaply built, with everything selling at premium prices.

A night's sleep, and I was checking in at Reeve Aleutian Airways for the flight to St. Paul on the Pribilof Islands. I found out I needn't have bothered being early, as this particular Reeve flight never left on time. Nobody bothered—if the plane didn't leave at 9:00 o'clock, it would leave at 10:00 o'clock, or later. I must say that the low-key, friendly atmosphere was restful. The delay gave me an opportunity of having breakfast with Gerry Wooldridge, a veterinarian from Fairbanks, Alaska, who would accompany me to the fur-seal hunt and prepare a veterinary report for the HSUS. Gerry was young and looked boyish, with straight blond hair and ready smile. We sat over cups of coffee while I told him about the Canadian seal hunt and he told me about the wonders of Alaska. Finally, we were called to board the rather elderly, four-engined aircraft that Mr. Reeve used for the Pribilof run, and within minutes were airborne and flying southwest down Cooke Inlet.

Miss Janice Reeve, no one else but the boss's daughter, was the chief stewardess on that flight and welcomed everyone. She handed me a map and I traced our flight path.

The Alaska Peninsula thrusts its bony finger out into the dark, grey waters separating the Bering Sea from the Pacific Ocean, and our route went straight down the middle of the mountainous range until we reached Cold Bay and its tiny landing strip. Settling back in my seat, I watched fascinated, as we flew over some wonderful country. The most impressive sight was the Valley of a Thousand Smokes, where many steaming volcanoes thrust their fire-blackened lips to the sky. Landing at Cold Bay was uneventful, but I found that we would be subjected to a long delay because weather conditions on St. Paul Island, our destination, were unsuitable for landing.

The small, dingy waiting-room at the airstrip had to be one of the most boring places in the world. Literally nothing but four walls and some chairs. Someone had pinned a colorful poster of New Zealand on one wall, and I remember wishing I was there in the sunshine.

One of the airport staff told me that powerful and large bears made a habit of raiding the garbage dump just beyond the airstrip so I collected my camera from the waiting aircraft in the hope of getting some pictures. After a windy and wet hour hiding behind some odious refuse— no pictures. The bears must have decided to go elsewhere. I looked out at the filth man insists on strewing around him, and couldn't blame them.

Airborne again, and we were swinging away to the northwest, out into the lonely, fog-shrouded Bering Sea. I hoped the pilot had good instruments, because if we missed the Pribilof group of islands there was an awful lot of nothing ahead of us. I can remember looking down on the cold uninviting water between breaks in fog and cloud and thinking that Mr. Pribilof, the Russian navigator who discovered the islands that bear his name, must have had quite a voyage.

It was in 1783, that Pribilof had begun searching for the breeding grounds of the Northern fur-seals that were known to swim north into the Bering Sea every spring. Prior to that time he had contented himself with killing the animals as they funneled through the narrow gaps in the Aleutian Chain, but now he sought a richer prize— the golden birthplace of the seals. After three years of searching the mysterious northern ocean, Gerassim Pribilof heard what to him must have been the most heavenly music: the throaty barkings of millions of seals from deep in the fog. Steering by that sound alone he would quickly have found the islands. Untouched by man until that moment, the masses of seals on the beaches must have been uncountable.

The Russians and their Aleut slaves would have swept down on the unsuspecting seals in an absolute orgy of brutal killing. And almost two centuries later the seal nursery would still not have recovered its tranquil peace.

Prior to the sale of Alaska to the U.S.A. in 1867, the Russians ruthlessly killed millions and millions of seals. Unchecked, the killing endangered the very survival of the species on at least two occasions. Early conservationists must have breathed a sigh of relief when Alaska was purchased by the U.S.A., but their relief was short-lived. American private enterprise exploited the animals even more ruthlessly than the Russians. Finally, with the seals perilously close to extinction, the U.S. Government took over management of the breeding areas. But even this was not enough. Seals were still being shot or speared from boats on the open sea by Americans, Canadians, Japanese, and Russians. This type of hunting, with its high proportion of seals wounded and not recovered, had to be ended if the fur-seals were to survive. Finally, in 1911, the U.S.A., Great Britain, Japan, and Russia concluded a Convention for the Protection of the Northern Fur-Seals. Pelagic (i.e. open water) sealing was prohibited to all except aborigines. The U.S.A., in return, agreed to give Canada and Japan fifteen per cent each of the annual take from the Pribilof herd.

I pulled my thoughts back over the centuries and into the aircraft once again, and began to pay more attention to the other people in the aircraft. There were two rows of double seats along the full length of the fuselage with a break on one side for the door and stewardess' station. I let my glance wander idly up and down the cabin and wondered why there were so many elderly ladies on the aircraft. St. Paul Island was a remote place way out in the Bering Sea, and certainly no vacation center. I caught Janice Reeve's eye, and she came over.

Janice told me that Reeve Aleutian Airways had a regular weekly schedule from Anchorage to St. Paul and return, and that they carried a good many tourists on every flight in the summer. They were people who had heard of the breeding grounds of the Northern fur-seal, and had the time and the money necessary to make a visit to them. There was a small hotel on the island—I knew that anyway—where the tourists were housed overnight. Out one day, back the next, and at a relatively high cost. It may have been at that point that I wondered if something similar could replace, at least partially, the hunt in the Gulf of St. Lawrence, Canada. I made a mental note to compare the two breeding areas in terms of tourist potential.

The "Fasten Safety Belts" sign flashed on, and the captain advised us over the loudspeaker that he was making his descent to St. Paul Island. We were in heavy mist at this time and I could see no sign of sea or ground. Lower and lower we sank and still the thick, clammy mist. I think everyone was a little uncomfortable before we finally broke through and had visual contact with the sea. A dull metallic grey, it looked cold and uninviting. Here and there white splashes showed briefly as some sea creature turned and twisted on the surface of that remote ocean.

Within quick seconds we were over land and I looked

down on the rain-soaked island that was to be my home for seven days. It looked dismal and uninviting. Nothing more than the weather-worn tip of a long-extinct volcano, the island was covered with soggy-looking, green vegetation. Pools of brackish water lay in natural hollows, and not a single tree was in sight. Here and there dirt roads marched purposefully across the land.

Dipping sharply to the left, the aircraft thundered over a scattering of houses, and I knew I was looking at the village of St. Paul, which shares St. Paul Island with an American Coast Guard Base and the seals.

The heart-stopping crash of undercarriage and flaps being lowered, and we were suddenly bumping along the runway. I looked out of the window at what must be one of the most primitive airports serving a regular passenger carrier. Just a bulldozed brown gash across the surface of the island. Off to our left was the Coast Guard fire engine, which presumably was meant to deal with any catastrophe that might happen. It didn't look capable of putting out a cigarette, and filled me with no confidence as we bumped to a stop.

It was raining, as is often the case on St. Paul Island, and I stood around for a while wondering what to do. An official of the American Government's Department of the Interior introduced himself to me and offered to drive me to the hotel. Thus, I met Ford Wilkie, a biologist who had spent years working with the fur-seals, and who was probably the foremost expert on these animals.

Because of the perpetual damp, and the rough roads, most vehicles on the Island are not merely undercoated on their undersurface, but over the exterior body, as well. I remember thinking that something similar would not be a bad idea in the part of Canada where I live, as corrosion is a real enemy of the motor car in our severe winters.

The village of St. Paul was not particularly impressive, merely two or three rows of houses accommodating some

123

600 souls. There were one or two government buildings, a couple of incredibly small canteens, a primitive theater and a tavern. This latter establishment, by some happy coincidence, was located right next to the hotel where I would stay.

There was the usual confusion and shuffling about. Baggage was carried hither and thither, and there was all the irritation associated with a large group of people arriving at one point at the same time. I have an aversion to such situations and leaving my baggage, wandered out of the hotel.

The people I saw in the streets were very interesting. Natives of the Aleutian Chain, they resembled the North American Indian. Dark complexions, straight jet black hair, high cheekbones and brown eyes. Dressed casually but well, they looked like men, women and children one might meet in Fredericton. I travel a great deal, and still tend to be amazed at finding that, in places remote from my home, other humans do not have two heads and eighteen fingers. I suppose it stems from a group superiority complex.

I scuffed my way through the unpaved streets that appeared to be surfaced with nothing but crushed volcanic rocks. The houses were the smallish, ranch-type bungalows common to every sub-division in North America. They looked reasonably well-cared-for and were laid out in neat straight lines. There were no gardens, presumably because of the very poor soil.

The hub of village activity that evening was of course the local tavern. Being a thirsty and dusty traveller, I felt it only proper to make my way there and introduce myself to the village celebrities. A single-storey building, it could accommodate perhaps fifty people in its one main room. In a small alcove was a juke box that blared songs, incessantly. A series of straight-backed booths ran down one side of the room, with individual tables and chairs on the other. They were all full of seemingly very merry islanders. I made my way to the bar and found that only beer was served. Drinking my beer from the can, there being no glasses available, I propped myself up against the wooden counter and looked around me. To know anything about the hunt meant knowing something about these people. I wondered what their reaction would be to a representative of an animal welfare society. I already knew that the economy of the island depended entirely on the seal hunt, and I could well imagine that the native islanders would not look too kindly on anyone who might challenge their way of life. In point of fact, as was the case with the Canadian seal hunters, they proved to be charming and delightful hosts. Quickly nicknaming me "Don't be Cruel", they accepted me into the life of the Island.

I made a special friend of an islander who rejoiced in the name of "Half-Can" (it seems that beer at the tavern was sold in full-size cans and half-size cans, and my friend had a taste for the malt brew in the smaller container). We were to spend some long evenings talking about seals, and drinking beer. He was good company and was possessed of a simple honesty that is becoming rare.

Later that night, I made my way back to the hotel and was provided with a room. I learned to my dismay that if I wanted to catch the seal hunt on the next day, I would have to be mobile at something like 4:00 o'clock in the morning. Appalled at the thought of such an early hour, I left instructions to be called.

The next morning, duly at 4 a.m., Ford Wilkie met me at the mess-hall where the seal hunters ate an early breakfast before going out to the killing grounds, and he was kind enough to provide me with rainwear. I had brought clothes that would meet with most normal situations, but the steady drenching wet so common on the island required garments of a more special nature—long, waterproof parkas, waterproof trousers, and heavy rubber boots.

On the Pribilof Islands, sexually immature males make up the bulk of the kill. These animals, three to four years of age, arrive on the beaches in late June, July, and early August. The sexually immature females arrive later. Seal pups, seals of less than three years of age, and seals of more than four years of age are not normally killed. Sometimes, however, females are deliberately killed in order to regulate the size of the herd. That pretty well was the picture, and now it remained for me to see what really took place.

I crowded into one of the vehicles that took the sealers and Government officials to the beaches where the young males would be found; these beaches are called "hauling grounds" by the local people. We bumped along the road, groping our way through the early morning misty rain, and stopped within sound of the sea. I attached myself to a group of hunters and followed them as they walked quickly over the matted green vegetation that covers the island, towards the sandy beach. Taking care to remain downwind of the seals, they raced to the water's edge, then quickly turned towards the unsuspecting seals and, moving rapidly, cut them off from the sea, the only means of escape.

I watched a scene of pandemonium. Several hundred animals had been trapped in this fashion and, desperate to escape from the frightening presence of man, milled around looking for an opening to the sea. The hunters were too careful to allow that to happen, however and, moving in on the seals, slowly forced them back from the sandy beach, across the jagged rocks that lay beyond, and up a low but steep cliff, and on to a flat field beyond.

Most of the seals were about the size of a large labrador dog, and resemble the seal most people would expect to see in a circus, balancing a ball on its nose. Their pelt was, however, much thicker than that of the species of seal commonly used as a performing animal, but the general appearance was the same. Here and there, there was a larger bull. These animals, not quite old enough, or not quite strong enough to gather about themselves a harem of females, often mixed with the young bachelors on the hauling grounds. Much more aggressive, they would turn and lunge at the driving sealers. These bulls were never killed, and the hunters took every opportunity of leaving them an escape route. This was difficult as the younger bachelors, seeing a hole in the driving ranks of men, would also lunge for the sea. But these younger animals were to be killed, and the sealers would quickly close ranks.

The seals moved, with a "dragging" motion. Unlike humans, who walk by putting one foot in front of the other, the seals seemed to stretch out with both front flippers, and then hauled their bodies behind them; they would then repeat the process. It was obviously very difficult for these animals to move any distance over land. Their distress from the driving was apparent to my eyes and ears. Their gasps and strangled breathing carried loudly over the still morning air. Occasionally, one of the seals would collapse and lie prone on the ground for a few seconds then, as the drive moved closer, would struggle to its feet and stagger on. This is torture, and nothing else. I saw several animals bleeding from the cuts they had given themselves on the jagged rock surface which they had crossed as they left the beach.

Other groups of sealers were driving the "raw" material of Madame's fur coat from adjacent beaches and some distance inland all of the seals were congregated in one large group of many hundreds. Their over-heated bodies steamed in the chill morning air. One man with a long wooden club and a large, bright tin-pail remained to guard the seals.

I noticed as I moved across the killing area that the vegetation was more lush, greener and thicker, and when I asked why this was so, I was told that the blood draining from the millions of animals slaughtered over the years had proven to be a very good fertilizer. Whenever I came across such a fertile spot on my travels over the Island in the ensuing days, I would feel a chill.

The seal hunt on the Pribilof Islands was vastly better organized than was the Canadian killing. Just a few men were involved, and over the years they had developed a highly efficient assembly-line-like technique. And that was the danger. So smooth was the operation that an observer could easily forget that beneath the veneer of civilized order was a very real tragedy for the animals involved.

It was time to kill.

Five husky men with heavy wooden clubs, perhaps about six feet long, stood to one side on the greenest spot of all. Guarding of the herd was taken over by a couple of boys, and the sealer with the bright tin-pail and club cut out from the main body of seals some ten of the animals and, moving behind them shouting and rattling the tin-pail on the end of his club, he drove them deliberately towards the killers. The seals, crowding together in their fear, moved in a compact mass towards the waiting clubs. I watched, unbelieving. Quickly, the five silent men with upraised clubs surrounded the gasping victims. For a brief moment, men and seals were silent and still, and shared a long glance together. The understanding that sport-hunters would have one believe flows from hunter to hunted was conspicuously absent. The seals made no effort to bow their heads for the clubs. They caught their breath and suddenly sprang for an imagined gap, but too late.

The swinging clubs whistled through the air striking at the mass of squirming animals. With quick accurate blows, first one and then another skull would be crushed. As individual animals desperately sought protection of a companion, the clubbers would stop, select a victim, and strike again. But the expert can miss. I watched as two animals received blows on soft parts of their body and collapsed to the ground in agony, their teeth snapping

128

and eyes bright with pain. Quickly, the men gave killing blows. Again, a pause in killing and then clubs were striking again. One seal, rearing back and opening his mouth in an enraged snarl, was struck full in the face, and coughing and spitting, bit savagely at the wooden club. Another terrified animal seeing an opening charged for the safety of the sea. One of the hunters chased him and struck at him with his club, and hit him across the back. The animal fell, then, to my absolute horror, the man stood watching the animal as it lay in agony for some ten to fifteen seconds before finally administering the killing blow. I was to watch this same man repeat that performance several times. And the killing proceeded with little variation from group to group of driven animals.

The dead seals were laid in neat rows of ten, and another group of men with sharp knives made a quick incision over each dying heart, and, baring still pulsing organs, stabbed with their knives.

The assembly-line technique rolled smoothly on. The *rippers* quickly loosed the pelts from head and flippers, and cut straight down the abdomen preparatory to the skin being ripped from the warm and bleeding carcass. The *bar-men*, using a spade-like instrument with two prongs instead of a blade, pierced the skull of each dead animal, and put their weight on the bar.

The *pullers*, three men, then attached forcep-like instruments to the loosened skin at the head of the seal and, with the aid of attached ropes, stripped the pelt from the carcass. Occasionally, the men would pull too vigorously and the body would separate at the neck. It was then the job of the *bar-man* to quickly thrust his spikes into the chest of the animal so that the pullers could, once again, have the purchase necessary for their job.

The *skin-boys*—boys on holiday from school—then moved in quickly and arranged the pelts in neat piles of ten for easy counting. *Stick-boys*, carrying small metal-pails

129

then removed the male sex organs from carcasses. These are shipped to China and used as an aphrodisiac. Sweeping along at the end of the operation come the *carcass crews,* picking up the remains of the seals in trucks and taking them to the bi-products plant.

That's it, that's the fur seal hunt. No glamour ... no nonsense about man against beast. Just dull, highly-organized brutality. Ugly, in the extreme, and as far as the vital needs of human society are concerned, totally unnecessary.

Later in the morning the tourists arrived. For the most part, they were neat middle-aged ladies, with just a scattering of husbands in tow. I felt sure that they would raise outraged protests against what was happening. Over they trudged, festooned with binoculars and cameras. I watched them, carefully.

At first they were obviously disturbed by the sights and the sounds of the killing. Here and there one would wince and glance away as the swinging clubs connected with bone and flesh. But, and to my sorrow, within a very short period of time they seemed to have accustomed themselves to what was going on. Chatting with the hunters and the Government inspectors, taking pictures and making notes, one would have thought they were at a football match. Later in the day I talked to some, and asked what they thought of the operation.

"Oh," one of them said, "it wasn't anywhere near as bad as I thought it would be. I don't think there was any cruelty to the seals."

For heaven's sake, what kind of human being is this?

One of my tasks was to take moving and still film, but poor weather encouraged me to leave the cameras in my hotel room and hope for brighter skies. I wanted to take pictures of seals enjoying themselves on the beaches, just being seals. Against this rather attractive background I would throw the killing into dramatic contrast. But I

130

needed sun. On the first clear day, because the happy scenes were more important, I went to one of the "rookeries".

No, one doesn't find rooks in a rookery on St. Paul's Island, one finds seals. What else?

The oldest and strongest bulls arrive on the more rocky beaches of the Island in April. There are several such areas and each one is called a rookery. Number one in the pecking order of bull seals commandeers the best spot, and so on down the line until the last and least attractive territory is claimed. Nature being what it is, this will still leave a number of other younger, or somewhat infirm, bulls who have not the strength to stake their claim to matrimony. These animals hang around the fringes of the rookery.

Towards the end of June the sexually mature females, oldest first, start to arrive and the territories become harems. Each harem is made up of one bull and an average of forty females. Some bulls have no harems because their territories do not attract females. I remember looking at some of these areas, and not for one moment could I imagine what it was in a particular territory that attracted a female seal. I remember wondering whether in fact it was the territory that attracted the female, or the appearance, or what have you, of the male seal concerned. Whatever it was, there was no doubt but that the best specimens had the largest harems. Considering that the male has to service some forty females and doesn't eat or drink from the time of his arrival in April, until he leaves in November, it's probably just as well! The pups are born between late June and late July.

Gerry Wooldridge and I spent a sunny afternoon at one of the rookeries with our cameras. He was taking still pictures for his own enjoyment, and I was taking movies and stills. It really was a glorious day, and I think back on it with a great deal of enjoyment and satisfaction. Surprisingly, for St. Paul Island, it was beautifully warm, and I was able to dispense with my heavy waterproof jacket.

The bull seals were readily noticeable. They are much bigger than the females and were almost always located in the centre of an admiring group of love-sick girls. A female seal is absolutely shameless. She lies there deliberately flaunting her charms at her lord and master and never seems to object to his most amorous advances! For his part, the male seal seems to exhibit a fair amount of indifference towards the girls. (Maybe there's a lesson for men in this.) Actually, I think the old boy is quite jealous, really. On several occasions I watched a female wander a little away from the harem. Immediately, the enraged bull would rush after her, pick her up bodily in his mouth and shake her. Suitably chastened, I suppose, she would then adopt her fawning position at the flippers of her master.

I wandered around the fringe of the rookery and found a lone bull that had the most violent of tempers and, perhaps as a result, no wives. I twisted the turret on my movie camera so that the wide-angle lense was in position, knelt down about twenty feet away from my irritable friend and proceeded to take film of him as he rushed towards me. I had forgotten that using a wide-angle view finder gave a different depth perceptive to the photographer, and when I judged the animal was about ten feet away, I lowered my camera and found several hundred pounds of angry seal practically on top of me and my head practically inside his gaping mouth. I hurriedly removed myself from his immediate vicinity. I thought that I would repeat this process a couple of times to ensure that I got good footage, and found the seal would always stop short of actual bodily contact with me. Giving every appearance of having one thought in mind—killing me—he would not, in the five or six times that I ran this sequence, actually harm me. I've often noticed this reaction with seals. Provided one makes no hostile move towards the animal concerned, and does not crowd him too closely, one is safe. I believe all the seals do is put on as aggressive a display as they judge necessary to ensure that they're not harmed.

I moved to another harem where a very large group of small black pup seals sat sunning themselves on the rocks. Black in color, they were much smaller than the harp seals, and totally unlike them. I suppose one might say they resemble black spaniel or labrador puppies. They seemed to show no fear of man, and calmly allowed themselves to be handled. Because their pelt has no commercial value these little fellows are not harmed by humans.

When I wasn't playing with seals, or, less happily, watching them being killed, I spent a lot of time with the native islanders. The community on St. Paul Island appears to be not a thriving one. The young people talk of leaving for the mainland. Many of the men leave the island at the end of the summer when the seal hunt is finished and seek employment for the winter. Often on fishing boats. This breakup of the family for long periods cannot but have harmful effects. Others, remaining on the island, make do with unemployment insurance. There is a desperate need for some other industry on this one-industry island. Fishing has been suggested, but little has been done in that direction, as yet.

It seemed to me, and I admit I'm no sociologist or anthropologist, that there was a definite hierarchy within the structured seal-hunt gang. The clubbers were number one, and so it went on down through the ranks, through the stickers, rippers, bar-men, pullers, skin-boys, carcass-crews and finally the lowly stick-boys. This social structure was clearly evident in the tavern where the clubbers would often hold court.

When I finally left the island, I presented a fairly lengthy report to the organizations that had sponsored my observations. As I always do in reports of this nature, I left it up to those to whom I reported to decide for one of a number of policies. In this case, as with the seals off the east coast of Canada, it was a policy of control or a policy of abolition, and the choice of which to demand was up to those who had commissioned my report.

The question of control, as always, is the easier to deal with. In almost every instance of animal abuse little attention is paid by those involved to reducing cruelty, Someone like myself, having some experience in the field, can always make suggestions that will improve matters. In my report I made the following specific recommendations for the 1968 harvest, if in fact killing was permitted that next year:

1. Shorten the length of the drives. Earth-moving equipment should be used if necessary to locate flat killing areas immediately adjacent to the hauling grounds.
2. Where hauling grounds have rocky surfaces, every effort should be made to clear smooth paths for the seals.
3. Groups of seals to be killed, and in front of the killers, should number no more than six.
4. Supervisors should ensure that the killers immediately despatch any injured seal.
5. New killers should be trained so that at least two groups of five men are available, one of which is resting while the other is killing.
6. Supervisors should be appointed to insure that as much suffering as possible is eliminated. This should be their sole function.
7. Research should be started on mechanical methods of slaughter, similar to those used in Federally inspected slaughter-houses, in an effort to replace the present barbaric killing method used on the fur seals.

And that was that, at least for a while.

The U.S. Department of the Interior was later subjected to a great deal of hostile criticism of the Pribilof seal hunt. Finally, after a series of meetings with myself, and the Humane Society of the United States, the Department organized a "Task Force", comprising the following people: Dr. Ford Wilkie, Biologist, Director, Marine Mammal Biological Laboratory, Bureau of Commercial Fisheries, Seattle, Washington—(Chairman of the Task Force); Mr. Mel Morse, President, Humane Society of the United States; Dr. Donald S. Balser, Research Biologist, Denuer Wildlife Research Center, Denver, Colorado; Dr. William Marshall, Biologist, University of Minnesota; and Dr. Galvan Pals, Veterinarian, Livestock Slaughter Inspection Division, U.S. Department of Agriculture, Washington D.C.

I was more or less seconded to the "Task Force" as an observer for the HSUS.

On July 17th, 1968, I arrived on St. Paul Island, for the second time, with Mr. Frank McMahon,[1] Field Director of the HSUS, who represented Mr. Mel Morse, the President of the HSUS. The "Task Force" was there: to determine the best method of killing large numbers of fur seals based on humane methods and aesthetics, taking into consideration the limitations imposed by conditions on the Pribilof Islands, including climate, terrain, costs, etc. It's a pity that some consideration was not to be given to stopping the whole shabby business, but maybe that will come later.

The "Task Force" had two main areas to consider. It would evaluate various killing methods, and try to improve present driving and killing practices.

The killing methods to be studied resembled something out of the Nazi Concentration Camps. These poor animals would be killed with carbon dioxide inhalation, electric shocks, captive bolt stunning, shooting, and clubbing.

The "Task Force" carried out most of its testing procedures in a large, cement-floored Government garage.

Carbon dioxide was the first alternative method of killing tested. Large tanks of this heavy, odorless, incombust-

[1] Frank, like myself, merely observed the "Task Force" at work. B.D.

135

ible gas had been transported to the island, and were ready in the garage. I already knew that exposure to this gas can produce in many animals unconsciousness and, if exposure is prolonged, death. Carbon dioxide is sometimes used in the slaughter of pigs and there is a tendency on the part of many people in animal welfare to assume that it produces a humane death, because pigs killed by this method are said to have died humanely. Personally, I have very grave doubts about the use of carbon dioxide. I have seen cats killed in humane society shelters by this method and observed, at first hand, the animals fighting and struggling for some considerable time before becoming unconscious. I know the scientists will say this is an hallucinatory phase that animals and humans go through before coming completely unconscious. I would answer it is extremely unwise to argue from species to species. O.K., so it doesn't distress or disturb human beings too much, but that is no guarantee that the same is so for other animals. Generally, I would think, the human being involved in the surgical use of this gas is well aware he is not going to be killed. He is, in fact, cooperating in what is happening. The same is certainly not true for animals. It might be that the surgical use of this gas in veterinary hospitals, even although it might not be very pleasant for the animal concerned, is acceptable because it produces good results. But unless the gas produces less stress to the animals than does clubbing, then it has no use or purpose on the Pribilof Islands. That is what the "Task Force" would hope to discover.

I leaned against the wall in the garage and looked around me. The scientists were busily preparing for their experiments. The seals were to be put in a large stainless-steel tank, which would be filled with carbon dioxide. A camera had been set up to record events, and pencils and notebooks were at the ready.

Lined up against one wall were eight or nine cages containing seals that had been recently captured. I felt immensely sorry for them. The whole business seemed so inhuman. I know, from personal experience, the bitter frustrations that come from being caught in an inexorable process. In my case, this has never cost me my life. In the case of the seals, they would be turned from living, feeling creatures into dead pulp. In all probability they would suffer enormously in the process. And there was not one thing they could do about it. How terrifying it must be for animals that undergo this treatment! The scientists have a fancy name for fear; they call it "stress". I watched those seals die and from now on I'm going to stick to the old word—terror.

I'm not going to try and present a scientific report of what happened, just a layman's eyewitness report: then I'm going to damn well offer some opinions.

Seal number one was put into the stainless-steel chamber, which was then filled with carbon dioxide. Everyone crowded around to watch. The floodlights of the camera were turned on and in the hush the worrying from the camera's mechanism sounded loud. Members of the "Task Force" and observers watched the seal as the carbon dioxide started to take effect. For one and a half long minutes the animal struggled on the floor of the chamber. Its breath vaporized on coming in contact with the carbon dioxide and I could see labored breathing.

Sickened, I watched the seal lose consciousness and, for the time being, its sufferings were at an end.

Several seals underwent similar treatment. The position of the stainless-steel box was changed occasionally and the timing was altered. The end result was that the members of the "Task Force" seemed to be unanimously of the opinion that there was not enough equipment on the island to adequately evaluate the effectiveness of carbon dioxide as a killing agent on the seal harvest. Anyone with a grain of intelligence could have guessed that fur seals can be

137

killed by this gas. Frankly, I am at a loss to understand how the representatives of a Government that can administer to the welfare of some two hundred million people, and make war in numerous places around the globe, can waste time and money dragging a lot of people to St. Paul Island, only to find that there was not enough equipment to evaluate what, after all, were relatively simple scientific tests. Someone had said that perhaps it was a deliberate waste of time. There does seem to be an inclination on the part of Government agencies to try to wear out their opponents. I can see this at work on the Canadian seal hunt as well.

I have already warned of the danger of arguing from species to species. I think it is not unreasonable, however, to note that when I was considering going to the Pribilof Islands as an observer, and knowing that carbon dioxide was going to be used on the seals, I did place myself in an atmosphere very heavy with this gas. I experienced an unpleasant, burning sensation in my eyes, something similar to the feeling one gets when exposed to tear gas.

The seals that had survived gassing were not to be released. I had hoped they would be, because I felt sorry for them. I suppose I could have forced the issue, but it would only have meant other seals being caught and used, and the end result, in terms of total animal suffering would not have been improved. From a purely scientific point of view, I could see the value of performing postmortems on all the animals that had been used in the experiments.

I walked over to the caged creatures which had not yet been killed, and kneeling down beside their cages, talked to some of them. I am sure they sensed my sympathy, for when I touched them they lay still and quiet, even those that had been subjected to the terror of the gas chamber.

Electric shock was the next method to be tested. This

method of killing is widely used for pigs, birds, and dogs. If it is to be called a humane death, an initial current must be passed through the brain in sufficient strength to cause instant unconsciousness. Death must follow without the animal recovering from this state.

The "Task Force" had got hold of a "seal-restrainer". A most vicious-looking instrument. It had been fashioned from a long wooden plank and a long iron bar with a hoop in the middle which fitted around the seal's neck. Catches held both ends of the bar down when the animal was firmly in place, and it had no hope of escape. It is quite obvious why this instrument was needed. The seals objected strongly to being handled and electrocuted and would bite if given an opportunity. I didn't blame them.

Struggling, the first seal was placed in the restraining device and electricity applied through a large pair of tong-like instruments, something like very large scissors; the electric current flowed through the insulated handles and into the animals *via* the sharp tips. The scientists found that the pelt of the seal formed an effective insulator to the passage of electricity. Because of this, and with the equipment available, it was not possible to pass an electric current directly through the brain of the animal using the ear to ear route.

There had to be *some* bare flesh on the seal that would permit the passage of electricity. The flipper to flipper route was used, and the scientists found that it was possible to stop the heart of a seal. After this, death occurred in an unknown lapse of time. The "Task Force" found it was also possible, using the mouth to flipper route, to render a seal immobile for a period of time, but these animals recovered.

What a bloody mess it all was! These poor, wretched animals had been tormented beyond belief, and it was quite obvious to me that again lack of equipment had demonstrated nothing else but that electricity could kill fur seals, and that the pelt of the animal was an effective insulator. I venture to suggest that any bright eighth-grader could have told them both these things.

The next killing instrument to be tested was the captive-bolt humane killer. This method of slaughter is widely used for food animals. Its main advantages are: safety for the operator; the virtual elimination of human error; and the elimination of the multiple blows sometimes required with clubbing. Provided an animal could be adequately restrained, the captive bolt did a really good job. As the name implies, no free projectile is used. What amounts to a blank cartridge is fired, and its explosive force channelled to the head of a bolt which is driven into the head. Buffers retain the bolt within the mechanism of the weapon and the operator merely draws it out of the animal's head after firing.

This particular killing instrument works well, provided some means of restraint is available. In so far as the fur seal hunt is concerned, there is the danger of substituting cruel restraint for cruel clubbing. This is hardly in the long-term best interests of the animals involved.

There were two seals left and these animals would be shot. Loaded into the back of a Government truck, they were taken to a grassy area well away from the village. Released, they scrambled at first towards the sea, but quickly stopped to rest. I watched one member of the "Task Force" lift his rifle and, aiming for the head of one of the seals, fire. The animal collapsed instantly and died without any apparent suffering. Crack, the other animal was down and again no apparent suffering.

There are obvious problems regarding shooting fur seals. The seals crowd together and projectiles that would not pass through one seal and injure another would need to be perfected. Men would have to be trained as skilled marksmen.

Drugs and tranquilizers, so I understand, were to have

been tested by the "Task Force", but it was considered that this was not necessary as some work had already been done by others. Personally, I was delighted not to have to witness this particular outrageous treatment of animals. There is no doubt but that seals can be killed by drugs and tranquilizers, and possibly humanely. But all such materials, so I was told, would leave a residue in the carcass of the animal. This would interfere with the use of the carcass for human and animal food, and its use in drug manufacture.

If—and I somehow doubt it—the use of drugs and tranquilizers proves to be the best method of killing large numbers of fur seals then, in my opinion, such a killing method should be adopted if the animals are not to be spared. Nobody eats seal-meat in any large quantity, and the manufacture of animal food and drugs from the carcasses could be discontinued. Neither item is of awesome concern to humanity.

After the "scientific" tests—if one could call them that considering the primitive and inadequate material available—the "Task Force" gave its attention to the killing method already in use—Clubbing.

I formed the impression, perhaps an incorrect one, that a majority of the "Task Force" was of the opinion that clubbing might very well be the most satisfactory way of disposing of these animals. I believe they may have thought there was no other practical alternative. If that is the case, then the whole wretched business must stop. As in 1967, I counted how many animals required multiple blows before they were rendered apparently unconscious or dead. The figure was the same—twelve per cent. Far, far too high. One other objectionable feature was the fact that there was a time lag between the killing of the first seal in front of clubbers and the killing of the last seal. The number of seals in front of the men obviously was a significant factor in this regard. The more seals there were, the longer the time lag.

One of my main criticisms in 1967 had been the length of the drives from the beaches to the killing areas. The "Task Force" undertook to recommend the drives be made as short as possible, and that a certain amount of "smoothing" of terrain be considered.

With one minor exception, all of my recommendations of 1967 on improvement of the harvest under present conditions, that is to say, with the continuation of clubbing, were accepted as worthy of adoption by the "Task Force". I only wish they had adopted my suggestion that the fur seal harvest be discontinued.

CHAPTER THIRTEEN

The 1968 Hunt and the Daily Mirror

I MADE several trips to Europe in 1967, as I was anxious to create increasing interest in the harp seals, particularly in the United Kingdom.

In common with many Britons, I had a childlike belief in the power wielded by the major daily newspapers. The *Daily Mirror* had the largest circulation of any newspaper in the country, and acting on the theory that one started at the top it was there I concentrated. If only I could get the *Daily Mirror* to expose 15 million readers to a "shock issue" on the baby seal hunt, I was sure the end of the killing would be closer.

Whenever I was in London I made a point of meeting Betty Tay the *Mirror*'s "animal expert". I made no bones about my intentions. I wanted her newspaper to cover the seal hunt, and she was the best contact possible. The fact that Betty was a great person made my job a pleasure. But had she been a terrible old dragon I would still have pursued her from one end of the city to the other.

This persistent wooing of a major newspaper might not make sense to some. But I had convinced myself that one day the Canadian Government would yield to hostile domestic and international public opinion. It was therefore important that as many people as possible be exposed to the facts of the hunt, and the *Daily Mirror* was the largest, English-speaking daily newspaper in the world.

One of the problems in dealing with people and organizations is getting someone to make a decision. If it had been up to Betty, I am sure the whole *Daily Mirror* staff would have done nothing else but fight the seal hunt. But Betty could not direct the newspaper to carry a "shock issue" on seals. Who in the whole complex structure of a huge organization could make such a decision? And that was not the only problem. It was likely that any one of several people could decide to send a reporter and photographer tripping over the ice floes of the Gulf of St. Lawrence. That being the case, within that management group, who was the most likely to look with favor on our cause?

I had watched a television program in Canada that showed Hugh Cudlip, the Chief Executive of the *Daily Mirror*, being interviewed by Pierre Burton, a well-known Canadian television personality. I had been tremendously impressed with Mr. Cudlip's very British sense of humor. He projected an image of warmth and humanity.

"Betty, do you think it would do any good for me to have a bash at Hugh Cudlip? If I'm going to get shot down it might as well be by the top man. Besides which, I think he's got enough imagination to be interested by the project." We were having a beer at the pub behind the *Mirror* offices in Holborn.

Betty thought I might be treading on a few toes, but it was my business. There was nothing for it but to type a letter to Hugh Cudlip as soon as possible. Flushed with enthusiasm, I commandeered Betty's desk in the huge and very busy newsroom. My letter to "Number One" might not have been ... hell, it wasn't a literary masterpiece, but it did the job. The *Daily Mirror*, because of my letter, because I met Betty, because ..., because ..., would have a reporting team at the hunt in 1968. Good things would happen for the seals.

Meanwhile, in Germany our valued friend Dr. Grzimek was locked in battle with the German fur trade. They thought it rather unkind of him to expose cruelty to Canadian seals! In fairness to the fur industry, Dr. Grzimek agreed to co-operate with them in further observations in 1968. A group of veterinary pathologists would perform autopsies on the carcasses of baby seals to determine the effectiveness, or otherwise, of the present killing methods. He contacted me. I agreed to organize transportation.

Although I believed the seal hunt was primarily an ethical issue, I was quite happy to have pathologists provide me with scientific facts. This was assuming, of course, that they would limit themselves to fact. It had been my experience in the past that some veterinarians, and I'm not speaking about Dr. Simpson, insisted on larding their reports with personal opinion. In an effort to head off a similar situation arising in the 1968 reports to the veterinary team, I sent out the following memorandum to ...

Dr. Charles F. Helmboldt (U.S.A.)

Dr. Bruno Schiefer (Germany)

Dr. Lars Karstad (Canada)

Dr. H. C. Loliger (Germany)

"The controversy surrounding the harp seal hunt in the Gulf of St. Lawrence, Canada, is so intense that I believe it is essential that we have, before the actual observations, agreement on the form of the report to be submitted by the team of veterinary pathologists, and on the nature of public comment the team members may make following their observations.

"Whether the seal hunt is, or is not cruel, is a philosophical decision, that, in all fairness, should be made by the groups sponsoring the observations. Obviously, their decision will be heavily influenced by the results obtained by the team, but other factors will have to be taken into consideration as well; the level at which animal suffering should not be tolerated by Society, the economic factors involved, etc., etc. These considerations, I respectfully suggest, are outside the highly objective science of veterinary pathology. I do not imply, however, that veterinary pathologists are less than capable of philosophical reasoning, but I do suggest, given that the scientific facts are available to all parties, that they are, by reason of their specialty, not more capable than the groups which are sponsoring the observations.

"By means of this memorandum I am requesting, with the greatest respect, the veterinary pathologists who are to form the team to restrict their reports to a presentation of autopsy findings. With regard to public statements made during and after the hunt, I would ask that the veterinary pathologists not state that the harp seal hunt in the Gulf of St. Lawrence, Canada, is, or is not cruel. The reports of the team should, and I am sure will be, given the conditions under which we must operate, a model of objective, scientific research. Organizations and individuals will, in the coming years, argue for and against the seal hunt, but the one thing that should be beyond arguments is the scientific report of the team.

"I sincerely hope that no one takes exception to the content of this memorandum. It is submitted to you with humility and respect. I have had a lot of experience with the seal hunt, and from past experience I know that it is essential to lay down mutually agreeable guide lines. Please write to me immediately if there are any serious objections in principle to the contents of this memorandum, and if by the end of February, 1968, no such objections have been received, I will assume that everyone is in agreement with my proposals."

In spite of my memorandum, and further exhortations to the scientific team while they were on the Magdalen Islands, a small amount of opinion crept into the reports. But, on the whole, I must say the veterinarians produced objective reports.

The hunt was to open late in March, 1968, some ten

146

days later than previous years. Well in advance I knew the seals were close to the Magdalen Islands. The telegrams went out and my party started to congregate at Grindstone. (We were keeping our noses—or at least my nose—to it, the pun permitted!)

Strictly speaking, I had not received permission from Dr. Grzimek or the fur trade to include reporters in my team. But, strictly speaking, I hadn't been told not to, either. And reporters, by definition, can do more for the seals than pathologists can.

Rather than list the eighteen or so people I had to juggle around in my two helicopters and two fixed-wing aircraft, I'll let them move in and out of the story as I write.

Conditions were not pleasant on the Magdalens. A partial thaw had set in, and the landscape was dripping wet. But, far worse, there was an element of deep hostility apparent in the attitude of the Magdaleners and some of the Canadian Government officials present. I do not think that I have ever felt so uncomfortable in my life. I really expected violence to erupt. It was much stronger than what I had felt in 1967.

In previous years I had, perhaps out of a sense of bravado, worn a large luminous cross on the back of my jacket. In this way I would be easily identifiable on the ice. I removed it while in Grindstone in 1968. Whenever I left my hotel at night I exercised caution. Perhaps I let the tense atmosphere inflame my imagination. But, I have a strong intuitive sense of survival, and my hairs were on end in the spring of '68.

My team was made up of veterinary pathologists and newsmen. And someone on the Island was getting at the vets. The newsmen were no problem. They expected to stick their necks out in order to get a story. The scientists, however, were in a different situation. They had no intention of getting themselves killed in order to provide Dr. Grzimek and the fur industry with a series of autopsies.

147

Bad weather restricted flying until the first day of the hunt, and for a while there was mischief for idle hands to do and nonsense for idle minds to be filled with.

During our forced grounding, the pathologists trotted around talking to many people. And, judging from their reactions, some of them must have been told they would die as soon as they stepped out of the aircraft onto the ice. I could just hear it. "Why, that ice is so rotten with this thaw that I don't think it would bear the weight of a silver dollar. You people are taking an awful chance going out there. That Brian Davies is going to kill you all."

Fred Beairsto was on the Island to help me keep my sanity. I guessed what I would be up against, and knew I would need a friend. Fred was a natural organizer who could take a load off my shoulders.

The night before the hunt opened. Fred and I were sitting in our room. Nothing very sumptuous. Just two beds and a couple of dressers. We kept getting delegations from the scientific side of our party. They would come down to our room to have "heart to heart talks" about the dangers of the morrow. Again and again we would explain to them that the hazards were more imagined than real. With their morale shored up, they would leave, only to be back very shortly with their confidence in tatters. This went on several times until, by about 3 o'clock in the morning, both Fred and I had just had as much as we could take. Finally, in desperation Fred told them:

"We'll take you out to the ice, you look at conditions, and if you don't like what you see we'll bring you right back to the island. Now, will you be satisfied with that?"

They would be. We hoped for the last time.

There is only one real danger at the seal hunt. That is, being left overnight on the ice. With an aircraft seat at one's disposal this danger was not great.

To present the situation fairly, I must write that it was obvious we could have done with more aircraft lift. There were eighteen people and only six seats—although in an emergency we could shove a couple of extra people into the fixed-wing aircraft. The veterinarians, however, were to be lifted off the ice first, and we had enough seats to get them to the Magdalens in one lift. That's about as safe as one can be. The newsmen would go in the second lift, and Fred and I would remain on the ice to be picked up on a third and final lift. The newsmen were big boys and were prepared to take events as they came. Fred and I after having been on the ice before knew the dangers were not as dreadful as people would have one believe, and in any event, we had a job to do and were prepared to take our chances. We had long ago decided that we were prepared to spend a night on the ice in order to achieve our goal.

THE FIRST DAY ON THE ICE

The ice that year had little snow-cover. Steel crampons were necessary (crampons are metal gadgets that clip to the boots and have sharp points that stick into the ice to provide traction). Everyone had been told to provide themselves with a pair. But of course, not everyone did. John Gray, my good friend from the *Montreal Star*, stepped out of the helicopter and in no time at all slid feet-first into a breathing hole. One of the seal hunters, as nimble as a cat, reached him in seconds to offer help. With his lower body and dignity severely dampened, John returned immediately to the hotel. That was the first mishap of the day.

I had chosen a large ice floe for the fixed-wing aircraft to land on. And our rather sizable group assembled at this point. The helicopters were then to move us, two at a time, to various areas of the hunt. But something went wrong.

I moved away from the landing point on foot to see a

149

few seals at close hand. The newspaper people followed me. The veterinary pathologists moved away in the opposite direction. All our plans to stay together as a group were about to crumble. We didn't mean to get separated, but a sudden change in wind moved the ice floes around in minutes and what had become two groups were suddenly out of sight and sound of each other.

In the meantime, one of the helicopters was transporting John back to base and was somewhere between me and the shore. The other helicopter had been placed at the disposal of a cameraman from the Associated Broadcasting Co., of New York, and was God knows where. The quick shift of ice had cut me off from the fixed-wing aircraft, which I couldn't even see.

Counting the pilots, there were twenty-two people involved in the shambles that was quickly being created. One group under control had now become two, and then four groups out of control with no contact with each other. Most of the people on the ice were completely out of touch with the all-important aircraft. I bet there are twenty-two versions of how it happened. This is mine.

I realized within minutes what had taken place. But the ice had moved so quickly I couldn't rectify the situation. I was most unhappy about the veterinary party. None of them had been on sea ice before, and they were entirely alone. I felt sure that no harm would come to them if they didn't panic, but my experiences of the night before were not such that I could convince myself that they would keep cool. At least, not all of them.

Still with me were Alan Gordon and Kent Gavin of the *Daily Mirror*, Farley Mowat (a writer), John De Visser (a photographer)—all of these men of considerable stature in their particular field—Fred and Dr. André Rousseau of the Canadian SPCA. Farley, nobody's fool and a man who knew the North, recognized we were in trouble as soon as I did, and it wasn't long before everyone realized

150

that plans had gone badly awry.

There was, however, still a job to be done, and with the exception of me everybody carried on. I was too busy worrying. I could imagine one of the veterinarians, having fallen through the ice into the frigid waters of the Gulf, standing surrounded by the rest of his pathologist friends and not knowing what to do slowly freezing to death. I'm sure now this didn't give enough credit for common sense to the men involved, but that is what was going through my mind.

I could see the Magdalens some fifteen miles away, and I wished I were there. In the distance a low range of hills, partially snow-covered, thrust their way out of the surrounding ice The wind increased in velocity and the floe we were on started to break up. We seemed to race across the surface of the ocean. Looking at land, a fixed point, made me giddy.

As well as moving quickly and breaking up, the innumerable ice floes, large and small, were separating. Stretches of open water appeared all around us. I felt very unhappy. If only I could be with the vets everything would be fine. Fred and the reporters could look after themselves.

In spite of my concern, I can remember one or two lighter moments. I remember Alan Gordon, notebook and pencil in hand, interviewing a particularly tough-looking Newfoundland sealer who shared our stretch of frozen sea. Short, tubby, and with cheeks bright red from the cold, Alan presented a humorous sight as he stumbled over the ice, clad in a borrowed coat that was several sizes too large for him. His cheap and totally inefficient crampons did nothing to help his dignity. Standing before his own personal seal hunter, Alan, in a funny English accent, interviewed at length. I listened.

The seal hunter was a bent little man. Unshaven and blood-spattered, he looked for all the world like a man of some seventy years. He was, in fact, only fifty. A brutally hard life in Newfoundland had aged him prematurely. He dutifully answered Gordon's questions.

"Yes, I will make about $300·00 for the week's work."

"Yes, I have a wife and children."

And so on. . . .

"I see sir," said Gordon. "Now, tell me: do you spend the money you earn on a holiday?"

The tough little Newfoundlander looked incredulous. As I watched him his jaw actually dropped. "Lord, sir," he said, "I spend it on my wife and kids." And with that he stomped off to another baby seal. Swinging his club at its head and missing his point of aim, he struck it a resounding whack on the back. The animal turned and twisted away. A second blow, on the mark this time, and our friend had moved a century away.

The whole sequence had been an unforgetable mixture of pathos, humour, and tragedy.

Pathos, humour, and tragedy apart, time was getting on and there was no sign of our helicopters. I was getting increasingly worried about the vets. I had taken the fluorescent cross off my back, and every time a likely looking helicopter flew near us Fred and I stretched the material out so that the fluorescent side pointed at it. It was our recognition signal for the helicopter pilots. Several machines flew their rattling course quite close to us, but they obviously belonged to the sealing fraternity for they paid no attention to our frantic signalling.

Pacing up and down the ice, I was seriously considering having a nervous breakdown, but, there was nowhere to have the damn thing. It was far too cold and unpleasant. Nervous breakdowns are a luxury to be enjoyed amongst civilized surroundings. I thought I had better save mine for another time. Something more practical was needed now.

Should I call for help. I knew the Government officials

would be delighted to see me signal an emergency. The story would go around ... "Davies gets into trouble on the ice, then wants the rest of the world to bail him out". I wanted to avoid that if at all possible.

I was faced with an agonizing choice. Wait until one of my helicopters turned up ... and there was little doubt but that one of them would, or give way to my concern for the scientific party by calling for help. In fact, the veterinarians had been provided with flares and were capable themselves of calling down rescue aircraft if necessary. Really, I suppose, I was more worried about their state of mind than anything else. It was my job to insure that they did their job, and if they left the Magdalens on the first available plane because of a frightening experience it would be my responsibility. Better for the seals to light the flare and suffer the consequent indignity.

I pulled out a flare and stripping off the striker drew it sharply across the fuse. Holding it at arm's length, I watched it burst into a brilliant crimson glow. Red smoke rolled over the ice. A circling Canadian Government, Department of Transport, helicopter dropped down immediately. Miserably, I walked over and told my story. There were no wisecracks or recriminations, just a genuine offer to help. Fred climbed into the aircraft and went to look for the lost animal doctors.

For my part, I turned towards a Fisheries helicopter which had also landed by now and waited for Mr. Dudka to clear the whirling roter. I could imagine I was going to receive different treatment from him. I told my story and waited. Predictably, Stan was less than gracious. "What do you want me to do. Prevent cruelty to seals or look for lost SPCA people?"—or words to that effect. Swallowing the angry retort that flew to my lips, I was about to acknowledge that I would prefer he look for lost vets, but it was not necessary. At that precise moment, and fate earned my undying gratitude, my own helicopter swung

153

into view and I signalled my pilot down.

Fred soon found the veterinarians. They had not been frightened, or even slightly alarmed. In fact, as I remember, they had not even missed us. I could have saved my flare and dignity.

Once things were again under control, I gathered everyone together on the large floe on which rested the fixed-wing aircraft. It was midday, and there were still a few hours of light left. I talked matters over with Fred, and we decided to ship the reporters back to land and work only with the vets.

Everything went smoothly during the remainder of the day. The veterinarians moved busily over the ice, prodding, probing, and taking pictures. Finally, late into the afternoon, we started to send everyone back to the hotel. Fred and I left on the last lift, and a tiring day was almost over. There was, however, a rather rough evening yet to endure.

I suppose I received the word around 7:00 p.m. It seemed that someone, I'm still not sure who, had decided to call what was virtually a public meeting in the lounge of the hotel. Brian Davies was to be taken to task for setting off a flare. I'd played that game before, and *they*, whoever they were, would find no meek lamb for slaughter.

The Department of Fisheries, the Department of Transport, the veterinarians, some of the reporters, the hotel staff, and, or so it appeared to me, half of Grindstone were gathered together in the lounge. I took my place in the middle of the room and waited for the action to start. It wasn't long getting under way.

It seemed that I had endangered the life and limb of several people, and finally had called for outside assistance, etc., etc., I must say that the representative of the Canadian Department of Transport was most reasonable in his comments, but I can hardly say the same for some of the other people present at that meeting.

154

I had first to decide whether or not I was even going to talk to this gathering. The veterinarians and journalists had a right to question my arrangements. I think the Department of Transport also had reasonable cause to enquire why I had called for help. But I could not imagine why I should explain myself to a large group that even included the hotel chef. The whole thing smelled too much of an inquisition for my liking. But, even if it was to tell some people that it was none of their damn business, I decided I would go along with the game.

I told the meeting that everyone in my party had been warned there was a possibility they would find themselves alone on the ice. That is to say, they would find themselves alone either as individuals or part of a group that was not accompanied by a representative of the "Save the Seals" Fund. All had agreed they would risk this possibility. Safety equipment that included signalling mirrors and flares had been issued to everyone. Each individual had been told to stay as one of a group and not to wander off. One person, I said, and I did not mention his name, had been issued a radio and told to remain with the veterinary party and to keep in radio contact with me. The gentleman in question had seen fit to allow himself to become detached from his party. Had he done as he was told, I could have established and maintained radio contact with the veterinarians. This would have eased the problems I faced. Assured that they were in no danger, I would merely have waited for my helicopter.

Finally, however, I accepted all the blame for our upset. I had taken a calculated risk. I had taken more people out on the ice than I could return to land in one lift. Things had gone wrong, but no one had been hurt. I claimed that the risk I had accepted was not unreasonable. The fact that helicopters are immediately available for everyone could not guarantee that the individuals concerned would not do something foolish. Having done something foolish, the main prerequisite was that someone was around to help them out of their predicament with an aircraft to take them back to land. When we needed one, we had an aircraft, even if I had to use a flare to get it.

Not one to ignore the lessons of recent history, I said that in the future I would limit the size of my party on the ice at any one time to ten. This would enable me, in an emergency, to get all but two persons back to land in one lift. As before, Fred and I were prepared to take our chances, and we would be the last two.

A fairly ugly situation could have developed. Alarmed by the overstated dangers of the morning, the veterinarians could have decided not to risk a further trip the next day. If this had been the case, I could have expected to lose the support of Dr. Grzimek. That was bad enough, but besides that I had a commitment to him I intended to honor. It had been clear to me at the very beginning that it was absolutely necessary for me to dominate the meeting. By the very nature of the position I held within the context of what was taking place, I was the centre of attention. Talking at length I held centre-stage and ruthlessly chopped down any opposition. I didn't like doing it, but the seals were more important than the bruised feelings of anyone present. The meeting came to a close, and I had prevented a mass defection from our ranks.

THE SECOND DAY ON THE ICE

Day two was grand for everyone but seals. It was beautiful sunny weather with the ice pressed against land by the wind, a solid mass for hundreds of square miles. And our flight arrangements worked almost perfectly.

The veterinarians spent the whole day on the ice and carried out hundreds of post mortems. The reporters, always difficult to please, had what I considered to be a

156

reasonable amount of time at the hunt, and I must say they were able to report at length and with excellent pictures.

Bad weather prevented further observations, and our coverage of the 1968 hunt was over.

Dr. Lars Karstad, the veterinary pathologist who was specifically the consultant for the New Brunswick SPCA "Save the Seals" Fund, later presented me with a report. It is too long to reproduce in detail here, but is given in full in Appendix A.

Dr. Karstad's report,[2] with the exception of one small item, was all that I could wish from a scientist. It was useful on two scores. One—it was now obvious that our vigorous campaign against the hunt had improved the killing methods. Two—I now had confirmation of Dr. Simpson's contention that some of the animals were killed under highly questionable circumstances. A small item that I did take some exception to was the sentence "I did not see any instance of intentional contravention or disregard of the sealing regulations". I felt it had no place in a scientific report as it didn't really mean anything. The fact that Dr. Karstad saw no intentional contravention of the regulations in no way indicates that there was no intentional contravention of such regulations. We corresponded on this item, and I quote from the last letter on the subject which I received from Dr. Karstad ...

"Now regarding your request that I modify my report, I would prefer to let it stand as it is, since for me to change it now would, or could, be taken as evidence that it was not a true report, to the best of my abilities. I will, however, give you permission to reproduce the report without the statement you wish deleted. In other words, I will not be changing my report but you will merely omit the statement 'I did not see any instance ... etc.'
Do not change the report otherwise."

[2] Attached as Appendix "A".

I gave some thought to Dr. Karstad's offer but decided to only reproduce the report in full.

Where was the action going to be following this hunt? In Montreal with the *Montreal Star*? In New York with ABC Television? No, the action was going to be in London with the mass circulation *Daily Mirror*. On March 26th thoroughly worn out, Fred and I landed at London Airport. I walked over to the newsstand at the airport and asked for a copy of the *Mirror*.

The front page jumped at me. A seal hunter with blood-stained hands and upraised club stood over an appealing baby harp seal. And the headline screamed: "THE PRICE OF A SEALSKIN COAT." Alan Gordon and Kent Gavin had done a fabulous job.

From time to time I have been told that the *Daily Mirror* played fast and loose with facts. From my own personal experience, I can say that it has as great a regard for the truth as any newspaper I have dealt with. Alan Gordon was never satisfied with anything I told him. He always double-checked what I offered. His story, which I read that morning was most skillfully written and scrupulously separated fact from opinion. Kent Gavin's pictures were equally telling. Indeed, his picture on the front page of the newspaper was as much the story of the seal hunt as were Alan Gordon's words.

There was a lot of angry criticism from the Canadian Government following the *Daily Mirror* story. I contend that Alan Gordon was more than fair to Canada's shabby baby seal hunt, in so far as fairness is possible with regard to slaughtering defenceless young animals.

The *Daily Mirror*'s presentation was not cold and clinical. A large daily newspaper is a living thing, a synthesis of all the varied emotions of the large group of men and women who create it and has a soul, a conscience, likes and dislikes. There could be no doubt but that the *Daily Mirror* did not like the seal hunt. Text, pictures, and captions had arranged themselves in such a way that the whole presentation left the reader numbed and shocked. The result was a massive indictment of the brutal butchery.

A spokesman in Prime Minister Pearson's office said that a splash feature-story in the London *Daily Mirror* criticizing the hunt was "quite reprehensible". "They are literally trying to ruin an industry," the spokesman said.

Mr. Pearson told the Canadian House of Commons that the *Daily Mirror* report was "unwarranted". "Steps are being taken to investigate the situation and to reply to the charges," he said.

Former Prime Minister John Diefenbaker asked whether Mr. Pearson would answer "the very frightening descriptions of the seal slaughter which have appeared in the British press". Mr. Diefenbaker also asked for a reply to widespread allegations that cruelty and brutality were practiced in the seal hunt and that stiffer regulations hadn't removed "a dark cloud over Canada".

The Prime Minister said he agreed that the report "does involve a dark cloud over Canada, however unwarranted that report may be". Canadian newspapers carried an item quoting unnamed Canadian Government officials who were supposedly studying the report. These anonymous officials commented that it appeared to be based, at least in part, on an incident two years ago in which the Government say seal hunters were paid to skin alive a seal pup for photographers.

The truth is that the *Daily Mirror* story made absolutely no reference to any picture that had ever been taken by anyone in the Gulf of St. Lawrence other than those taken by their own man at the 1968 hunt. It is quite clear that the only reason for releasing such a comment was to attempt to discredit the newspaper and anyone who sought to end the seal hunt. It was really no answer at all, just a deliberate and vicious attempt to create in the mind of the public an incorrect appreciation of the true circumstances.

The same bright Government officials also said that "sealing had a definite conservation value in that it cuts the number of fish eaten by the migrating harps and hoods". That was true enough, but the same Government officials should have known, and in fact I am sure must have known, that the migrating harps and hoods present no known danger to the commercial fishery off the east coast of Canada. I will deal with this later in the story.

It was the same old situation. There was—and is—absolutely no reasonable justification for the seal hunt to continue in Canada. To placate an outraged British public, charges of faked films and destroyed fisheries came flashing from the press mills of the Government. The harm done to Canada's "image" by the *Mirror* story had to be undone.

The Fisheries Minister had something rather special for me. Apparently Davies had to be "got" at all costs. And Ottawa started sending out what appeared to be form-letters over the Minister's printed signature. Of course, a number of them found their way back to me. One to Pat Shaw read as follows:

Ottawa
April 17, 1968

Miss Pat Shaw,
Shaw Studios of Dancing,
7 Adelaide Street East,
Toronto 1, Ontario

Dear Miss Shaw:

I wish to acknowledge receipt of your letter of April 9, 1968, regarding the annual seal hunt. It is with regret that I notice how you have been influenced by unfair and untrue propaganda made by S.P.C.A. officials and others who are definitely against this annual operation.

It is most unfortunate that so many people like yourself give credence to such reports and refuse to acknowledge statements made by competent persons who have observed the hunt in the Gulf of St. Lawrence and have made reports on their observations.

I would refer particularly to two of the independent observers who witnessed the hunt during the 1968 season: Dr. E. A. Costello, veterinarian from the Department of Agriculture, who states in his report: "At no time did I witness an act of cruelty", and Dr. R. A. Jones, of the Royal School of Veterinary Studies, also an expert on sealing matters, who states in his report: "I saw no intentional cruelty at all while we were on the ice. No animal was flensed while conscious. These animals were certainly dead within seconds of the flensing process beginning, as the major arteries were soon severed."

Furthermore, other independent observers, such as Dr. Grzimek and Dr. Schiefer, both of Germany, are contradicting openly in German newspapers statements made by Mr. Brian Davies. They wish to disassociate themselves from such statements; they quote such statements as being "wilful misrepresentation for malicious political purposes". They have asked German newspapers to apologize for connecting them with the statements made on the hunt by Mr. Brian Davies. They condemn newspapers for not giving their readers an objective report. Dr. Grzimek has advised German news agencies that all animals had completely smashed skulls before they were skinned. He also acknowledged the success achieved by the Canadian Government in having trained seal hunters using a special club. Such statements are quite contrary to the malicious attack made by Mr. Brian Davies and some of his associates.

I would hope that judging from the reports stated above you will agree that suitable legislation has been introduced and is being enforced by the Canadian authorities to protect the annual seal operation.

Yours sincerely,
H. J. Robichaud

161

I immediately sent a copy of this letter to Dr. Grzimek and Dr. Schiefer. Extracts from their replies follow:

June 6, 1968

His Excellency
The Minister of Fisheries
Mr. H. J. Robichaud
Ottawa
Canada

Your Excellency,
    ... I want to correct you, that I personally am not an "independent observer", as I was not in St. Lawrence Gulf during the seal slaughter ...
    ... Mr. Brian Davies and the New Brunswick SPCA were very helpful in organizing the journey for the scientists sent out by us with the financial help of the German Fur Traders Union. Until now I have not heard any publications of Mr. Brian Davies which are in disagreement with the facts of the scientists or with our press notice on this matter, of which I enclose a copy.
    Therefore I would like to ask you to keep to real facts in official letters of your Ministry.

Yours sincerely,
Grzimek

Mr. Brian D. Davies
Executive Secretary
New Brunswick Society for the Prevention
of Cruelty to Animals
P.O Box 1011
Fredericton, N.B./Canada

Dear Mr. Davies:
    ... There is no question, that Dr. Grzimek was not an observer of this year's hunt, as everyone knows ...
    ... In summary, I want to declare again, that obviously your and my opinion of the seal hunt are different

ones. You should take the liberty of saying and writing your thoughts on the seal hunt, but the same liberty applies to me. I am not going to say—and I never did— that you, Mr. Davies, are giving wilful misrepresentations for malicious political purposes.

I would hope, that this letter might explain the discrepancies.

With kind personal regards

Yours very sincerely,
Bruna Schiefer, Dr. med vet.
Privatdozent

I immediately wrote to the Prime Minister of Canada asking that the false statements concerning my colleagues and myself be corrected. As is so often the case when dealing with Government, nothing happened.

Later in the year, I received from Dr. Grzimek a copy of a letter he had received from the Fisheries Minister. Dated June 11th, 1968, it read:

I wish to thank you for your letter of June 6th, referring to a letter which I addressed to Miss Pat Shaw, 7 Adelaide Street East, Toronto 1, Ontario, in reply to her letter protesting against the annual seal hunt in the Gulf of St. Lawrence.

I at once accept your statement and am pleased to learn that you were not an independent observer during the 1968 hunt in the Gulf. I am also pleased to know that the scientists who did observe the hunt this year are in a position to state that the endeavors of the Canadian Government have succeeded in avoiding nearly all the cruelties which have been reported by observers in the previous year. I can assure you that your letter, together with a copy of the testimony of experts who were sent to the Gulf of St. Lawrence, will assist in recording the real facts regarding this particular operation.

Yours sincerely,
H. J. Robichaud

Without doubt this is the most cynical letter I have ever read. Cynicism lay in what he did not write rather than in what he did write.

As far as I know, no recipient of Mr. Robichaud's first letter ever received a corrected version.

As was the case with the earlier *Weekend Magazine* article, the *Daily Mirror* story created a deep public hostility to the seal hunt. Thousands of people wrote to me, and many of them have stayed with the issue forming, in the United Kingdom, a solid base of support for our work. One twelve-year-old girl sent me a letter that moved me deeply. She wrote that she had cried when reading of the killing of baby seals and, not knowing what else she could do, had immediately gone into the streets to collect signatures on a petition she had put together using the Kent Gavin picture and some scraps of paper. She told me not to reply to her home address, but to write c/o her Grandmother as her mother did not like her doing anything for animals. I could picture that lonely little girl with her desperate concern and eager eyes and hands on the cold pavements of some English town.

Alan Gordon's story and Kent Gavin's pictures had been a huge step forward. But, as the year wore on and I continued working for the seals in North America and Europe, it became increasingly clear that the Canadian Government, while seriously embarrassed by the seal hunt, was not yet prepared to call it quits. Further blows were needed, and it was hardly likely that the *Daily Mirror* would carry a similar issue in 1969. I would have to look elsewhere for the massive support the seals needed in this next year.

CHAPTER FOURTEEN

The 1969 Hunt and Paris-Match

EARLY in 1968, Patrice Habans, correspondent for the French magazine *Paris-Match*, had flown to Canada to report on the seal hunt. Arriving too late for the actual killing, he had researched the subject in Montreal and travelled to Fredericton to interview me. His idea at that time was a story on me, my family and our animals, with the seal hunt as the background. Since that time Patrice and I had corresponded rather spottily, and nothing had materialized in the magazine—France's most influential.

In late November, or perhaps it was early December of 1968, I was in Paris after visiting several "action groups" that were busily establishing themselves in Europe. These groups were militant fighters against the seal hunt, and I felt it was my job, even though they were completely autonomous, to impress upon them that their activities must not, in any way, reflect an anti-Canadian sentiment. I warned them that if they did not scrupulously confine their attentions to kicking the seal hunt rather than Canadians they would be doing a grave injustice to the truly humane Canadians who wished for its abolition.

I called *Paris-Match* and within a few minutes Patrice was in my hotel room and we were discussing seals. He was keen to photograph the hunt, and his dark handsome face became animated as he talked of making sure he took the most dramatic pictures.

Another important *Paris-Match* staffer now entered the plot: Marc Heimer, one of the magazine's senior writers. Marc is clever and cool. He has a deep respect for animals, and he wanted to see his magazine play a part in exposing the shocking seal hunt. We talked for some time on the telephone and, as I remember, the arrangement was that some of my material would be used for a story to be carried early in 1969.

Well satisfied with the day's work, I continued my journey home via London, where I met with my *Daily Mirror* friends to see if they might be interested in reporting on the 1969 hunt. The *Mirror* didn't want to send another team to the ice but they would hold a watching brief.

As though testing public reaction, *Paris-Match* first ran a story about me. It had a good response. Then came a story about the seal hunt itself using mostly my pictures and background information. *Paris-Match* was totally overwhelmed by reader response. Thousands of letters poured into the Paris office. French radio and television seized on the issue, and foreign publications almost fought over republication rights. Without catching breath, *Paris-Match* immediately ran another article with "pretty" pictures of seals and a selection of letters they had received. Some of these letters were from the most influential people in Europe, people such as Princess Paola of Belgium and Bernard Calle (Canon of Notre-Dame, Paris). In Monaco Princess Grace signed a petition addressed to the Canadian Government. And many French-speaking children took up the cause of seals with vigor. One French organization, the "Maison des Jeunes et de la Culture", sent me an incredible 60,000 letters and signatures in support of a sanctuary for seals.

Of immediate benefit was the appeal *Paris-Match* published mentioning our Paris bank account number. The response was most encouraging. By the time interest passed its peak, we had raised some $13,000 for the seals. And letters at the rate of 300 a day poured into my Fredericton office. *Paris-Match* had, in my opinion, done more than just expose the brutality of an obscure Canadian seal hunt. The astounding response demonstrated, I am convinced, that together the seals and *Paris-Match* had awakened in the hearts and minds of many French people a new and dynamic interest in all aspects of animal welfare. In the process, France had given the lie to the long-held Anglo-Saxon belief that Frenchmen do not care about animals. From one source or another, by the end of 1969 we had received from France some 80,000 communications regarding the seal hunt. On a per capita basis this far exceeded the response we had received from any other country. A warming thought to me has been the conviction that through this new interest animals in general in France have benefited immeasurably.

We were swinging along. And 1969 looked as though it might be a good year for seals.

The management of *Paris-Match*, with barely enough time in hand decided after the tremendous response to the stories they had already carried, to send Patrice and a writer, Bernard Giquel, to cover the 1969 hunt. I agreed to arrange facilities for them.

Bernard, a member of *Paris-Match*'s New York Bureau, was known to be a very sensitive writer, and some of his friends wondered, privately, if the brutality of the seal hunt might not be too much for him. I met with Bernard several times in New York before the actual hunt, and he determined for himself that he would do the story.

In March, Fred Beairsto, Patrice, Bernard, and I were in Moncton, New Brunswick, waiting for the seal hunt to start. We had two helicopters and a fixed-wing aircraft and were well equipped to do a good job.

It had been a strange year with respect to ice conditions. Water temperatures in the Gulf had not fallen low enough for sea ice to form until early March. The normally huge floes were nowhere to be seen, and the available ice was weak and located in the Northumberland Straits. (This latter is a narrow strip of water between Prince Edward Island and New Brunswick in the southeastern corner of the huge inland sea.)

A day or two before our arrival in Moncton, the seals had been blown close to the shores of Eastern New Brunswick and a new element entered the scene. Men who had never seen a harp seal before straddled their snowmobiles, small machines something like motorcycles that run with a track and skis, and roared out over the ice to kill some 2,500 baby seals before an alarmed Fisheries Minister ordered a halt. Ignoring the Fisheries Minister's demand that killing be stopped, these men again lined up on the shores of New Brunswick ready to defy authority. There might have been a confrontation between the government and the landsmen had a shift in the wind not blown the seals beyond the landsmen's reach.

THE 1969 HUNT: THE FIRST DAY

Opening day of the hunt saw Fred and me up early— very early, I think about 3:30 in the morning. It was bitterly cold outside, and I looked out of my hotel window onto a frozen world. Snow, feet deep, lay everywhere. The night sky, free from clouds, was superb. Millions of stars danced, diamond bright, against the black velvet background. I tried to open the window. It was frozen shut. I turned back into the overheated room and prodded Fred into wakefulness.

A while later, weighed down with equipment, which included flares, emergency rations, signaling mirrors, crampons, cameras and lots of warm clothing (Fred, true to form, again had twenty-eight sweaters!), we were down in the lobby of the hotel and ready to go. At this point

I decided to be sick.

Rushing off to the men's washroom I vomited, repeatedly and painfully. My face turned grey and a film of sweat covered my forehead. That was all I needed. 4:00 in the morning, the start of the seal hunt, bitterly cold, and I was feeling ill. Jovially, Fred told me that I was holding up the taxi that would take us to breakfast.

"Good Grief!"

I crawled miserably into the waiting taxi and was whisked off to a greasy little restaurant. Fred and the three pilots ordered large helpings of bacon and eggs with toast and coffee. I just shook my head when the waitress looked at me inquiringly. I wanted to do nothing else but sit quietly in a corner. The thought of food absolutely revolted me.

When the steaming plates arrived on the table, I was, within moments, rushing past an alarmed waitress and out to the street where I was wretchedly sick.

"Today is going to a real bad one," I thought to myself.

My stomach, I am sure, stayed behind in Moncton, but the rest of the party and what remained of me presently arrived at the small airfield we were operating from, situated some seven or eight miles outside the City. Then we met problem No. 1 for the day. We were outside the building; the aircraft were inside and nobody had a key. And it was getting damn cold. The door, however, quickly yielded to repeated kicks and we were in business.

I had decided to move our whole operation to P.E.I. in order to be closer to the present location of the seal herd. Patrice and Bernard were already there, having crossed on the ferry the night before. Their plan was to drive up and down the coast road looking for landsmen going out to the seals on snowmobiles. I hoped I could find our two friends when we arrived, and I remember wishing I had pressed harder for them to stay with me. I had already learned bitter lessons about allowing my group to splinter, in which case communication breaks down almost immediately and it is very difficult to regain direction of events.

By 9:30 in the morning we had reached P.E.I., and our helicopters landed on the outskirts of the small coastal town called Summerside (shades of Jack and Jill). The ships and seals, still in the Northumberland Straits, were about fifteen minutes away. We were ideally situated to do our job.

We were on a snow-covered field lying between the town and the frozen beaches. Wearily, I climbed down and started towards the nearest houses to telephone the hotel where Patrice and Bernard might be located. I wanted them, and fast. There was work to do for seals.

I trudged through the deep snow wishing I were dead and reached a small frozen stream that lay in my path. Veteran of several years of clambering over floating sea ice without so much as a wet foot, I jumped. And I jumped short.

Plunging through the ice up to my thighs I fell forward, cruelly wrenching my leg. Soaking wet from the waist down and gasping with pain, I started to vomit again. I lay on the snow for about five minutes before I could walk.

I spent the rest of the morning being very ill while Fred located Patrice and Bernard. Finally, around noon, we were all together and ready to go. The seals were close to shore, and we soon reached the hunt scene. Several blood-streaked ships pressed in on part of the herd. Small black figures scurried across the floes at the end of long bloody trails that reached back to these ships.

I stepped out and looked at a now familiar scene. The same brutality and destruction.

Leaving the others, I walked some little distance from where we landed to make my own private peace with the animals. I can still vividly remember this moment. I stood and looked around me. The seals were there, in their thousands. The ice was a jagged pattern of great beauty.

The sky was blue; the sun was warm and white cloud puffs drifted from one end of the horizon to the other. I thought of all that had happened since 1965. Jack and Jill, *Weekend Magazine*, all the lusty battles across Canada and through Europe, the countless good-hearted people who had strained to the best of their abilities to help the seals. And up to that point, we had all failed. I felt deeply moved, and searched my mind for words. All I could think of was a simple "I am sorry".

I turned. Patrice, distinctive in his bright blue jacket, was busily taking pictures of a group of three hunters moving rapidly across an ice floe with swinging clubs. Bernard, with no dramatic moment to freeze on film, stood quietly watching. His shoulders slumped dejectedly and, meeting my eyes, he merely shook his head with an expression of absolute distaste on his face.

Still feeling ill, I lay on the ice for some time; but the hunt was moving, and I had to move with it. Bernard and Patrice must be shown everything. Fred and I knew the character of the hunt could change from moment to moment, and certainly from day to day. On one floe the killing could be quick and clean. On another, the most blood-chilling and brutal of scenes might take place. Our friends from *Paris-Match* must see it all.

We moved to the vicinity of a small, rust-streaked ship from Halifax, Nova Scotia. In the distance I could see mother seals nuzzling closer to their young and looking in puzzled anxiety at approaching hunters. Then the hunters were among them and adult seals, terrified beyond all endurance, fled into the water. There, anxiously bobbing up and down, they watched the massacre of their babies. Now and again a small white seal would struggle towards the illusory safety of a shaded patch of ice. It was always too late.

These hunters worked their way towards us, and one man, dressed in denim trousers and a thick tartan shirt, crossed to our floe. For a moment this man rested and talked with us. He said he had the flu and felt sick. Within short moments, he was killing again. There were several young seals in our immediate vicinity, and he stood before each one in its turn cursing and raging for perhaps half a minute before bringing down his club. This man did not find it easy to kill.

The hunt moved on, and Fred and I sat on the ice for a while. It really was a lovely scene, and we discussed the possibility of tourism replacing the hunt. Within a few hours of major population centres like Montreal and New York, the seal herd presented a unique opportunity for many people to observe large numbers of wild animals at close hand. I looked across at a stretch of open water and saw twenty or thirty adults swimming gracefully from one end of the *lead* to the other. Moving in almost orchestrated precision, they flowed across the surface. People suffering from the tensions and frustrations of urban living in densely populated cities of northeastern North America could find wonderful moments of peace here, I thought.

Later in the afternoon, our work on the ice completed for the day, we flew back to P.E.I. and our hotel.

It is time to introduce the Honorable Jack Davis, Canada's new Minister of the combined Department of Fisheries and Forestry. Mr. Davis had replaced Mr. Robichaud who had been sent to the Senate.

The new Minister had swooped in from Ottawa, taken a look at the seal hunt in his jet helicopter, and at 9 o'clock that night was prepared to speak to the press.

Mr. Davis had earlier publicly warned the sealing industry that if there was cruelty in the 1969 hunt he would give very serious consideration to ending the killing. He had avoided defining "cruelty", however, so he really had not said very much.

I hadn't eaten for about two days, and was getting very hungry. My stomach had decided to stop being sick, and

I was looking forward to a meal before the Minister's press conference. Mr. Davis and his retinue, however, were filling every nook and cranny of the hotel restaurant: they seemed set to keep on eating forever. At 8:30 that evening, Fred and I finally managed to slip behind an empty, crumb-covered table, but the hotel's kitchen had completely collapsed under the assault of ravenous politicians and civil servants. By 9:00 our dinner had not yet been served, and it was time to hear what the Minister had to say.

The press conference was held in a large basement room in the hotel. The newspaper reporters were seated around a long wooden table at the head of which sat Mr. Davis, and one or two of his advisers. The television camera lights were on and pointing at the Minister when I arrived. I sat quietly on a chair in the corner of the room and listened. I didn't hear anything to give me one iota of comfort. The same arguments for continuing the seal hunt were used. Thousands of people needed the money. Fishing in the Gulf would be impaired if this herd of hungry animals were not controlled, etc.

The silliest comment that night was from a local reporter who had heard the Minister pointing out that the seals would die of natural causes (old age perhaps) if they weren't killed by man. This brilliant gentleman, in all seriousness, suggested to the Minister that "the seal hunters, then, are actually being kind to the seals by clubbing them to death so quickly".

Bloody fool! I could only sit there and shake my head. The same argument could also apply to you, I thought.

After the press conference, Fred and I finally had our dinner and very late that night went to bed. I had hardly got beneath the sheets when there was a rap at the door. It was a television reporter, waving a bottle of beer.

"Are you the Brian Davies who is causing a lot of fuss about seals?"

I said I was.

"Could I interview you? I must warn you that after listening to the Minister I am not too much in favour of your point of view, and I'll have some hard questions to ask."

Tired, and discouraged by the Minister's recent remarks, the officious attitude of the interviewer irritated me. For the first time, I declined to take part in a television interview.

Before falling asleep I reviewed what we had achieved during the day. We had taken the French journalists to the hunt and shown them all that they wanted to see. Whatever else might happen, we had done *that* job.

A surprising thing today was the marked absence of females defending young. I had always seen this phenomena in the past and really was at a loss to explain to myself or to anyone else why it had been absent. Day two, however, was to be a different story.

THE 1969 HUNT: THE SECOND DAY

The second day of the hunt stands out in my mind for two events. I met the Minister on the ice, and I saw the shocking sequence of events that were to later anger so many people through the pages of *Paris-Match*.

Patrice and Bernard had gone flying off again to see if they could find landsmen going out to the seals. Fred and I, knowing full well that two days of the seal hunt are never the same, were out on the ice early in the morning ready to report and record.

I had hardly orientated myself when I realized something incredible was happening. Large numbers of mother seals were staying on the ice to defend their young from the hunters. Everywhere I looked I could see irate adult seals lunging at men. The killers worked in pairs: one would attempt to distract a female with a swinging rope

174

or club so that his companion could dart in and grab her baby by its hind flippers. If successful, this man would drag the young seal some distance away to club and skin at his leisure. Again and again I saw this happening, and it was a horrifying experience for anyone even remotely concerned about animals. What the seals suffered as this took place I could not imagine.

Suddenly, with a roar of jet engines the Minister's group landed on the ice about a quarter of a mile away from me.

I thought to myself: I have had enough of this. I am going over to see him.

There was a fair amount of broken ice and open water separating us, and I suppose it took me about twenty minutes to pick my way around the worst stretches in order to get to Mr. Davis. When I arrived on the large ice floe on which his party had landed, it became apparent to me that neither he nor the people he was travelling with could see the seal hunt I know. The seal hunt that I observe on my flat feet and on my own.

There were two or three large helicopters and what appeared to be scores of people chasing around. I could only see four or five seal hunters, and each appeared to have half a dozen onlookers practically sitting on his shoulders as he went about the business of killing. Not unnaturally, the two mother seals who had decided to stay and defend their young ones on this particular floe had been left untouched. No one present could possibly have reported accurately on the seal hunt after observing such an unreal situation.

I was upset and angry when I finally sighted Mr. Davis, who was talking with a couple of his Department officials. One of them was Stanley Dudka who has appeared in this story before. I walked up to the Minister and introduced myself. Without delay I launched into my story about the scores of female seals defending their young and asked him to put a stop to the killing.

175

For a long moment we looked at each other and then, turning away from me, Mr. Davis stared down at the ice, his face reddened, and looking up, he said, "I can't make a statement on that now."

One of his assistants asked me to demonstrate what I meant. I walked to the two mother seals that were still on that floe with their pups and, as gently as I could, tried to touch the babies. Furiously, the mothers turned on me and I backed away. Swinging around to the Minister, I looked at him. He made no comment and turned away. My audience was obviously over, and I headed back for my helicopter.

On the way I noticed a female seal lying across the slashed carcass of her baby, angrily defying a hunter's attempts to reach it. Here were the shots that Patrice, who had recently joined us, needed to take. I hurried across to him. Moving quickly into position he started taking photographs. Bernard, for his part, apparently was sick of watching slaughter and sat on a protruding piece of ice looking dejected. I waved to him and motioned towards the scene that was taking place, but he merely looked up and shook his head. I joined Patrice.

The hunter, a young Newfoundlander, was dressed in green overalls and wore a red and yellow woolen hat. He had clubbed the young seal, bled it with a swift knife thrust, and had driven the hook on the end of his rope deep into the animal's head preparatory to dragging it away to a central skinning point. Before he could do that, however, the mother had arrived on the scene and, raging, had hurled her 500 pounds at him. Abandoning the dead seal, rope and club, he had retreated to a safe distance. Now he wanted to retrieve his victim.

Again and again he attempted to drive the seal away, but she would have none of that. Every time he advanced towards the dead pup, the mother would lunge towards him and throw herself across the pathetic little carcass.

Top. The sealing vessel Theta ploughs through heavy ice in the Gulf. The author "hitched" a ride on this ship in order to observe the 1966 hunt. *Bottom*. A young harp seal, perhaps 5 days old, is crushed by the passing vessel.

Canada is not the only country which organizes seal hunts. The same thing happens on the American Pribilof Islands. *Top*. These seals are very different from the Seal Harp but they too are clubbed to death. *Bottom*. The hunters collect together the rewards of their work while the young boy finds a joke in cutting out part of the carcase.

Sickened by the cruelty of the hunt many people are working to see it abolished. *Top.* Dr. Elizabeth Simpson being floated across an open stretch of water. It was here that our fisheries officer guide "sank" in 1966. *Centre.* The well-known model Celia Hammond sees at first-hand the living animal which provides the luxury of a seal skin coat. *Bottom left.* The author and Dr. Simpson on the ice. *Bottom right.* The author's children on the ice in 1969. Even children can travel to see the seal herd.

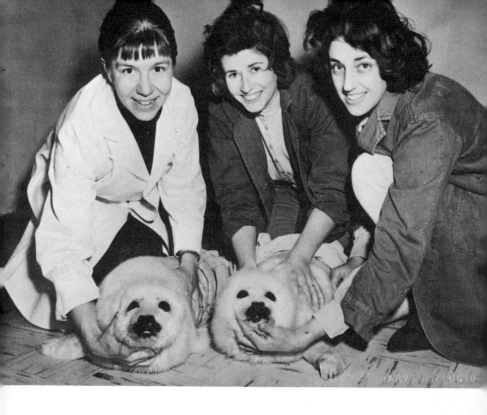

Top. These are the two pups, Jack and Jill which the author took home, with the three ladies Liz, Rita and Joan who devoted so much time to rearing them. *Bottom left.* Stan Dudka a sympathetic fisheries officer with a seal pup.

Shouting and cursing, the man redoubled his efforts, and Patrice recorded on film a sequence of photographs that have to rank as the most barbaric portrayal of inhumanity to animals on record. Finally, cursing, the killer gave up and plodded across the ice to other animals.

As he passed, he told me that by the time he came back the mother would have gone and he would get the skin.

"Damned old cow. She's crazier 'en hell," he said.

I turned, and in the distance I could see P.E.I., where all the trappings of modern civilization lay. Yet here, just a few miles away, was barbarism.

We started to work our way back to shore, and my helicopter put down beside a group of some six hunters—landsmen. They had walked out two miles from the shore of P.E.I. and were busily "getting themselves a few seals". They had no real idea of how to deal with the animals they killed: one came over to ask me, of all people, if I knew how to skin a baby seal.

I talked to three of them and found out that far from being the penniless shorehunters that the Canadian Government would have one believe depend on the seal hunt they were in fact men of quite comfortable circumstances. One was a member of the Royal Canadian Airforce, one worked in an office, and the third was a schoolboy.

Calling it a day, we flew back to our hotel. Patrice and Bernard were satisfied with the material they had obtained. They both felt that they had enough for an excellent article and that there was no point in staying any longer. That night they left for the mainland.

Events started to go from bad to worse for seal hunters shortly after. The female seals, through some unexplained mechanism, had been able to hold back giving birth for some ten days, until the late ice appeared in the Gulf. As a result, at this time the baby seals were too small to be of any real economic value. I heard one buyer tell landsmen that the hundreds of pelts they had were of no value.

"You might as well throw them away," he said. *Hundreds of seals had been uselessly killed.*

Still on P.E.I., and keeping our eyes open, Fred and I put down beside one group of landsmen and listened while they discussed their problem. It seemed low prices or not they wanted to kill seals. Just at this time, however, the Government helicopter landed, and Stanley Dudka got out to talk to them.

He told them that seal hunters from the ships were prepared to agree to a temporary halt in killing if the landsmen would also agree to stop. Stan went on to explain in great detail that if this was done the mother seals would have an opportunity of feeding the babies for several days and the resulting growth in the young animals would make their pelt much more valuable. Everyone agreed that this was a tremendous idea. And the hunt was called off for a while.

I listened to Stan and shook my head. I could think of nothing more bestial than stopping the brutal massacre merely to allow the uncomprehending mothers an opportunity of fattening up their pups for the clubs and knives of the killers. What sort of people were we dealing with?

The hunt did resume briefly, but was quickly stopped again by Mr. Davis who, perhaps, was disturbed by the public uproar that was fast reaching boiling point in many parts of the world.

THE 1969 HUNT: EPILOGUE

Fred and I were convinced that the magnificent spectacle of the harp seal nursery in the Gulf of St. Lawrence was something that could be used to the cultural advantage of mankind. Whenever I had suggested this to people in authority, I had been laughed down.

"It's far too dangerous to take people out there," I was told.

"Dangerous, be damned" was always my retort, and 1969 was going to be the year when I would prove it. So convinced was I that the dangers were grossly overrated I decided as a demonstration of my belief, to take Joan and the children, Nicky, now twelve, and Toni, now eight, to see the seals. Fred also decided to let his wife, Dixie, and his six-year-old daughter, Karen, share in the experience.

Fred and I paid personally the expenses involved, except for the helicopter time, which was given to us by *Paris-Match*.

Flying out over the ice, we landed on the very fringes of a small group of seals. Wives and children climbed out and thoroughly enjoyed themselves for some hours. Baby seals in their dozens were gently stroked, and the female seals, as though sensing there was now no danger, objected hardly at all. Occasionally, one mother would get rather possessive of her baby, but then it was just a question of sitting quietly for a few minutes until she calmed down and accepted our presence.

Toni became very much involved with one young seal and said, "They won't kill this one, will they, Daddy?" I couldn't give her an answer.

Nicky, a "man", was less obviously emotional, but he enjoyed being with the seals and often talks of the experience.

Other Canadian children should have an opportunity of seeing Canada's wonderful seals at firsthand. I hope this book encourages sponsorship of such tours, by business and/or government.

The seals would rather share their ice-home with kind human beings than be clubbed. How wrong it is to destroy them for worthless bits of fur-trim. Why not travel to this naturally beautiful area and appreciate nature as it was, perhaps one million years ago? It never fails to sadden me that those in power in Canada can, so consistently be blind to the real value of the seal herd.

A few weeks later the *Daily Mirror* carried a picture of Nicky and Toni cuddling a baby seal. Their caption captured a magic moment, perfectly. The *Mirror* said:

"The man with the upraised club and the bloodstained hands is gone. In his place come the children, ready with a laugh and a cuddle.
Times have changed for the baby seals of Canada.
For March is the culling season. Last year 50,000 seals were slaughtered. The *Mirror*'s Kent Gavin took the memorable picture on the right in the Gulf of St. Lawrence. The picture caused a storm and helped him to become British Press Photographer of the year. This year Fisheries Minister Jack Davis has halted the massacre.
The result is seen in the picture below. In March 1969, a seal has trust, not fear in its eyes as it plays with 12-year-old Nicky Davies and his sister Toni, aged eight.
Their father Brian Davies, led the fight to stop the hunt. Now he wants to turn the Gulf into a sanctuary. So that scenes of horror on the icefloes will never take place again."

THE 1969 HUNT: THE AFTERMATH

For his part, Fisheries Minister Jack Davis was making encouraging noises. Reporting to the Commons on his weekend inspection of the Gulf seal hunt, Mr. Davis was reported to have said he was convinced that supervision was effective and the suffering of young seals kept to a minimum. The newspaper article I read, went on to quote Mr. Davis directly:

"I could not help asking myself whether the hunt in the Gulf of St. Lawrence was really necessary in the first place.
"If we could convert this unique happening into an annual tourist attraction it could contribute materially

to the economy of the Atlantic region.

"I think we must therefore explore the possibility of the Gulf of St. Lawrence being declared a sanctuary for seals with the hunt itself being limited to international waters in the North Atlantic off Labrador and Newfoundland."

This was exactly what I had been saying all along. For the rest of 1969 I desperately tried to develop the tourist theme, but it has not been an easy task. Government cuts in expenditures have resulted in little help from the Department of Fisheries and Forestry. The International Fund for Animal Welfare, inc., the new organization I now work for, and which carries on the fight for the seals, will organize a small symbolic tour to the ice floes in 1970. We hope that the interest we create will encourage "commercial" tours to the seals.

CHAPTER FIFTEEN

The Canadian Government Reacts

FURIOUS over the continuing fight I had been waging against the hunt, the Canadian Government decided on an *inquisition*.

On Tuesday, April 15th, 1969, exhausted after the seal hunt and two gruelling three-week lecture tours around Europe, I faced the Canadian House of Commons Standing Committee on Fisheries and Forestry, in Ottawa, for five bitter hours.

Until that day, I believed that my rights as a Canadian citizen were, for the most part, fairly well protected. Now I am not so sure, because on April 15th, during that five-hour period in the witness stand before the House of Commons Committee on Fisheries and Forestry, I learned that my rights, even within the shadow of the Peace Tower, could take quite a beating. On that day, as the Committee enquired into the seal hunt, I felt the whole weight of Canada's Parliament come crashing down on me, and I learned that Parliamentary committees can, and do, ask a witness any question that comes into their minds—regardless of how relevant or irrelevant it is to the matter being studied, or how personally embarrassing it may be for the witness.

I learned that evidence based on rumor and hearsay could be used against me—and was.

I discovered, to my cost, the committee has unlimited powers. It need not answer to any court for its actions, and it is truly above the law which most Canadians live by.

I found the committee has the power to destroy a man's reputation and get away with it if it so desires, and I believe that in my case the House of Commons Standing Committee on Fisheries and Forestry wished to do just that.

And I learned there was not a thing I could do about it.

The Committee was hostile towards me from the very start because of my efforts to ban the seal hunt. The hearing was an inquisition. There was every attempt through innuendo to destroy my character. The following are extracts from the Official Minutes of the Committee, which are available from the Queen's Printer, Ottawa, Ontario, Canada:

MR. MCGRATH (*Committee Member*): You cannot interrupt me today because you are a witness, but I can interrupt you. That is the difference, you see.

This was the first incredible stinging backhand from a committee member as I sought to defend my position.

MR. LUNDRIGAN (*Committee Member*): May I ask the witness if he is deriving any monies indirectly from his involvement as a result of contributions made by certain people who might want to contribute to the SPCA movement and his campaign to end seal fishing in the St. Lawrence? In other words, from people who have a genuine interest in animals, who are animal lovers, and who might have an extra dollar in their pockets? May I ask the witness if he is gettting any of this—if it is creaming off in any way into his own personal account?

Furious, but holding back my temper as best I could, I answered with a simple, "No."

MR. LUNDRIGAN: I raise the question, Mr. Chairman, because a number of people have made the observation —I certainly have had it made to me, as a member of Parliament—that the witness is in actual fact not only conducting a campaign against the seal fishery in the St. Lawrence but is also doing a very healthy job of making a very good personal investment. In other words, he has a vested interest in it, and it is more than seal fishery. I think it would be very nice to clear up this point because I am sure that there are many people nationally and internationally who would like to know whether in fact it is a matter of its being a business venture. Certainly if it is then it sheds new light on the situation and I would be able to look at it from a different point of view.

If a person wants to conduct a campaign against anything, a campaign, let us say, for killing people, he is getting well paid for it, and there are those in the world who make a living from this kind of business, I understand; and that makes for underground movements. But if he can get a living from it then it creates a different impression.

The question I want to ask Mr. Chairman, is whether, in fact, there are any monies coming into the SPCA from people outside Canada?

Some seventeen Members of Parliament faced me, most of them with hostility in their eyes. Long tables had been set up in an open-ended square, and the chairman of the Committee, Mr. Guy Crossman, sat at the head-table with me to his right. I looked across at Mr. Lundrigan who sat to my left.

"How many questions are you asking there?" I said.

MR. LUNDRIGAN: That is the question you have to answer. The rest of my remarks constituted a statement.

"Frankly," I said, "I think your remarks are unworthy of you." Actually, I didn't really think anything of the

184

kind. The type of comment he had made was the sort of statement I would expect from someone like him.

MR. LUNDRIGAN: Mr. Chairman, on a point of order. I am not going to accept this kind of contemptuous attitude on the part of the witness. I am saying, as a Member of Parliament, that I have received an indication that the particular witness we have before us has a vested interest in the business. That is why I ask the question. Now he is saying that my remarks are unworthy of me. My remarks, therefore, are unworthy of the people whom I represent, and I will not accept this kind of contemptuous attitude on the part of this gentleman.

Therefore, Mr. Chairman, my question is: Are there any funds coming from people outside Canada, specifically in England, which are used to finance the efforts of the witness we have before us.

I had a sheet of paper in front of me on which I had written *Keep Cool,* and I looked at it carefully before answering my inquisitor. But, there is a time and place for everything, and I judged it was time to hit back.

Allowing some anger to creep into my voice, I said, "I do not know what your question is, but if you are intimating that I am ..." Mr. Lundrigan cut me off.

MR. LUNDRIGAN: I am asking, Mr. Chairman—and this is not information at all—if any monies are coming from outside the country and being used by the witness to carry on his campaign, and if these funds are coming specifically from England? This is my question.

More angrily I answered: "All the funds that come to the 'Save the Seals' Fund are used for this work. All of the funds are audited at the end of the year...." Mr. Lundrigan stopped me again.

MR. LUNDRIGAN: Mr. Chairman, this is not my ques-

185

tion. The witness, Mr. Chairman, should be reminded that he is under oath and should answer the questions. I am not asking about the auditing of the account. I am asking are there funds coming into the SPCA from outside the country and being used by the witness? And are any of these from England? That is the question and it is a very simple one.

I started to ask what all this business was about, but was once more cut short by Mr. Lundrigan.

MR. LUNDRIGAN: Mr. Chairman, on a point of order. The witness is not aware that he is before a parliamentary committee and that there is a question before him.
MR. MCGRATH: He is not addressing the annual meeting of the SPCA now.

That was too delicious to miss. I snapped back: "That is quite evident." And then I went on to say: "Yes, there is money coming from England to the New Brunswick SPCA which is used ..." At this point Mr. McGrath cut me off.

MR. MCGRATH: I am going to raise a question of privilege and ask that that remark of the witness, which was contemptuous, be stricken from the record. I reminded him, in supporting my colleague, that he was not addressing the annual meeting of the SPCA, and he said very sarcastically that that was quite evident. This has been in keeping with the generally contemptuous attitude that he has been showing this afternoon.

To give the Committee its due, I would have to say that my attitude during the session was defensive, although I deny I had been contemptuous. I knew the sealing issue was an extremely contentious one and that the members of Parliament who were arrayed against me, as it were, came for the most part from fishing-orientated constituencies. Regardless of the rights and wrongs of the matter, they could expect that their constituents would be happy to see Brian Davies given a sound drubbing by their "local boy made good".

I believed that some of the members of the committee would use their parliamentary immunity to destroy my reputation and to further their own goals. I knew that I had no recourse whatsoever. I could not go to a civil court and take action for libel or slander.

I do not argue the members' rights to defend the seal hunt or to call me before them. But I am convinced they should not use what could only be called, in retrospect, fascist methods.

MR. HOGARTH (*Committee Member*): I have a supplementary. What is the largest donation your fund has received within Canada?

I answered that it was one thousand dollars.

MR. HOGARTH: Was that one donation, or is it an annual donation?

"The thousand dollars was the largest and it was not repeated, at least I don't think so," I said.

MR. HOGARTH: It was not repeated?

"I do not think it was," I answered.

MR. HOGARTH: Who donated that?

The original arrangement with Miss H. M. Copp, who donated the $1,000·00, was that her name would not be divulged in connection with the money. She preferred to do her work for animals with no fanfare. I tried to explain to the committee that I felt the identity of the donor was confidential and that I preferred not to answer the question. Mr. Hogarth appealed to the chairman and demanded an answer.

THE CHAIRMAN: We will allow it.

I then gave them the information they required.

I was shaken by my experiences before the committee. Immediately afterwards I convinced myself that I couldn't go through anything similar again and that if the committee kept up the pressure by continually calling me before them I would quit fighting for seals.

During that period, as the events of the committee meeting went round and round in my head at night, I can remember feeling that a murderer in court would have received more protection than I did under the rules of Parliament.

I believed that a majority of the committee wanted to see the seal hunt continue. I was sure that many of them felt that if they could destroy the reputation of the person most closely identified with the anti-seal-hunt cause —me, that is—then the cause would be lost.

I think a good example of this was during a period in the questioning when I was quizzed about flying lessons I had started to take from Fredericton Aviation. This Company had rented the SPCA a helicopter in 1967, and I had asked them if the SPCA could get a reduced rate. The answer had been no, because the Canadian Government Department of Transport regulations do not permit such a thing. Seeking to get the best possible deal for the SPCA that I could, I then asked if I could be provided with a cut-rate on flying lessons. The work-load in connection with both animals in New Brunswick and the seal hunt had increased, and I thought that flying to remote areas of the Province in order to get my work done in a shorter period of time would help me get more done. If I could fly myself, it would have been of benefit to the New

Brunswick SPCA, but it didn't come out like that in the questioning.

> MR. CROUSE (*Committee Member*): Were there any other arrangements whereby you have personally benefited, because this is what we are talking about, personal benefits which should or could be added to your personal income as a result of your activities? Were there any other—well, sometimes we politicians are accused of accepting kickbacks so I will use that word—were there any other kickbacks to you personally as a result of your activities?

"In aviation?" I asked.

> MR. CROUSE: With regard to aviation, with regard to the entire field of work in which you are engaged; that is the destruction of the Canadian sealing industry.

Gordon Petrie, a Fredericton lawyer and personal friend of mine, had agreed to represent me at the hearings. Gordon had no particular brief for the cause of the seals. But he is a brilliant young lawyer, and I was happy when he agreed to represent me.

After the committee hearing, as we talked together in our hotel room, Gordon said, "I was appalled and shocked at what went on. I didn't believe that sort of thing could happen in Canada."

We were talking about the events at the very beginning of the committee hearing when I told the chairman that I wanted to be represented by legal counsel. Normal in any court of justice, this simple request was pounced upon by some of the committee members who made it appear as though I had something to hide.

> MR. MCGRATH: May I ask him why he feels he needs legal counsel? We have been hearing witnesses in committees . . .

THE CHAIRMAN: Gentlemen, shall we deal with the requests in order?

MR. MCGRATH: Mr. Chairman, I put a question to the witness, if you do not mind. I would like to ask him why he feels he needs counsel at this time?

And later ...

MR. MCGRATH: This has to do with the question I directed at the witness at the start. Why does he feel he needs counsel?

Gordon, who was sitting next to me at the time, leaned over and whispered in my ear. "In other words, guilty until proven innocent," he said.

MR. LUNDRIGAN: Mr. Chairman, could I ask a question of Dr. Ollivier? (Dr. P. Maurice Ollivier, parliamentary counsel.) In the event that our friend does get the consent of the committee to have legal counsel does it mean on the advice of his counsellor my question might be refused and that I cannot proceed with my line of questions?

DR. OLLIVIER: No. You can ask any question you want and the witness is obliged to answer.

They did finally allow me to be represented by legal counsel, but Gordon was advised by Dr. Ollivier that if he said anything he might be thrown out of the room. All my lawyer could do was sit quietly by my side and give whispered instructions.

I can remember on one occasion hearing him whisper, "I didn't know this could happen. I feel embarrassed at being a lawyer."

Later, he was to say in an interview with *Weekend Magazine*: "After this particular hearing I felt there was abuse of the powers of the Members of Parliament for personal or other reasons. They had abused their positions.

There was abuse of parliamentary privilege and particularly there was abuse of a Canadian citizen."

A couple of committee members did make some attempt at coming to my rescue.

MR. WHELAN (*Committee Member*): Can I suggest something? I think there has been 12 or 14 supplementaries allowed before a person who has been given the floor is allowed to proceed with his line of questions. This is way off base. I never sat in a committee where we went so far off base in the seven years that I have been a member of Parliament.

I directed a mental "thank you", at Mr. Whelan.

THE CHAIRMAN: Do not be so critical now. Let us do the best we can to revert to our normal procedure.

And later ...

MR. ANDERSON (*Committee Member*): Once more, before starting questioning, I will repeat what I said earlier—that this is just a terrible way to run a committee. You are not responsible, Mr. Chairman; we decided to run it this stupid way, and I really do object to it.

THE CHAIRMAN: I am in the hands of the committee.

MR. ANDERSON: You are. I am sorry that the committee puts you in the position of running a committee in this crazy manner ...

I'm not at all sure that the committee was being run in a *crazy* manner. There was nothing crazy about the methods that were being used to destroy me. I was left in no doubt as to what some of them thought of me. For example, to shake me and it could have been for no other reason, I was made to give evidence under oath while another witness was trusted and permitted to answer questions without being sworn.

Gordon later remarked that under this type of committee procedure questions can be asked in the form of an accusation. "This is very dangerous," he said.

The fact that other witnesses can appear before the committee and, protected by the rules of Parliamentary procedure, can express extremely damaging opinions without benefit of the injured party's legal counsel cross-examining, is another extremely unjust feature of the Canadian Parliamentary Committee system.

For Example:

MR. STADT: This I will say in English so that there is no misrepresentation of what I say: I think the film (made on the seal hunt by Brian Davies) is contentious. I think the film stinks and I think the man who did that film not only sold himself but all of us in all of the country—purely and simply.

MR. HOGARTH: All right. What authority does the Society for the Protection of Cruelty to Animals (Sic) in New Brunswick have to establish sanctuaries for animals? And was there a resolution of the board that brought about this determination of yours or the society that they were going to establish a sanctuary for seals?

"I'm not sure," I said. "The resolution was in 1966."

MR. HOGARTH: I asked you was there a resolution?

"Would you just let me make my point?" I appealed.

MR. HOGARTH: Just answer my question: Was there a resolution?

"I cannot answer your question now," I said. The resolution had been passed in 1966, and this was 1969 and I just did not remember the exact wording.

MR. HOGARTH: You do not know whether there was a resolution or not?

192

"If you will allow me to speak, I will explain." I would have told him that I just couldn't remember at this late date.

MR. HOGARTH: I am just asking you if there was a resolution?

And later . . .

MR. LUNDRIGAN: Mr. Chairman, I am not going to accept this kind of advice. I did not ask for advice from the witness, although he seems very capable of giving it. I want to ask him a further question on this very same point. Does he, with his very broad knowledge of the situation and in-depth study of it, know for a fact or at all that young seals have been known to have drowned this particular season.

"I do not know for a fact," I said.

MR. LUNDRIGAN: Therefore would you say that perhaps the statement by the minister (of fisheries) and the statement by departmental officials is perhaps out of order?

I wasn't going to be caught by that one. "I would not care—first of all I have the greatest respect for the Minister." I was going to give a careful answer, but . . .

MR. LUNDRIGAN: We are all aware of your great respect for the minister.

"Would you let me finish my answer?" I asked.

MR. LUNDRIGAN: No, I will not, Mr. Chairman. I asked the question and I want a yes or a no answer. I am not interested in the witness's respect for the minister of fisheries . . .

It will be as well to note, at this point, that Mr. Lundrigan and the Minister were in opposing political parties.

MR. MCGRATH: I am very interested in that question, Mr. Chairman, because my father went to the ice for many years. Many Newfoundlanders did go seal hunting. I see no evidence of this having affected him.

Gordon Petrie's remark about this particular line of questioning was: "I could see that certain members of the committee were definitely emotionally involved with the seal hunt—if not personally."

I had charged that the seal hunt brutalized the hunters. I believed that then, and I believe it now. How could any man involved in an occupation that saw him beat to death some one hundred and twenty-five young animals a day not be, to some extent, brutalized by what he was doing?

During the hearing, the film that Ralph Kay had taken in 1967 came in for its share of abuse.

MR. CROUSE: I have one or two more questions. The film, Mr. Chairman, also showed that the men stepped aside to show this whitecoat (baby seal) alive, still wiggling, while the man stood there with his foot on it. Now we are concerned with the truth which we did not get here this morning, this afternoon, and we are not getting this evening—the truth of the method by which seals are killed. I submit that from sunup until sundown these man have a task—they must kill as many seals as possible in order to provide for their livelihood, and they have not any time, Mr. Chairman, to stand around and watch a seal wiggle while they stand there with their foot on it.

Does the witness still insist that this film was not faked?

"Yes, of course," I answered.

Towards the end of the meeting I was getting very, very tired. Exhausted before I had even appeared before the committee, my five-hour ordeal had sapped my strength and energy.

The questions had come fast and thick and had reached a point where I had several questions, statements, and accusations in front of me.

And I rebelled.

"Mr. Chairman," I said, "I have been asked three questions so far. I have not had an opportunity of answering any of them. I would like to make this quite clear, sir, I don't know what you can do to me if I refuse to go along with this charade of justice—you may put me in jail if you wish—but I demand the opportunity of answering each question at length before further questions are put to me."

MR. MCGRATH: Mr. Chairman, on a point of order. This is not a charade of justice. This is a parliamentary committee carrying out an investigation under a reference by the Parliament of Canada. I do not think the witness has the right to make that type of statement. I ask you to rule accordingly.

THE CHAIRMAN: I think that when questions are asked he should have the right to answer and then—

MR. MCGRATH: This is not a charade of justice. That is how the witness has just described the committee.

THE CHAIRMAN: That is right, but I would ask the members of the committee to state their questions and let him have a chance to answer each question as it is asked.

MR. MCGRATH: Mr. Chairman, I have just raised a point of order and I ask you for a ruling. The witness has just described this committee, which is operating under a reference of Parliament, as a charade of justice. I ask that the witness withdraw that statement.

THE CHAIRMAN: Well, I think you are right. I would assert on that.

Grimly, I kept my mouth tight closed. I would see them all in hell before I would withdraw anything. Perhaps sensing my mood, the chairman didn't wait for any answer from me but moved swiftly on to the next question.

It was obvious to me towards the end of the day that

195

the committee really wasn't finding out anything. I am convinced that they had hoped to find some criminal activity of mine, but lacking this they really didn't know why else they had me there. I am sure a majority of them were totally opposed to the stopping of the hunt and were not really interested in any arguments I might have in an opposite direction.

MR. BORRIE (*Committee Member*): What I am really trying to get at here, Mr. Davies, is that I really do not understand your thinking behind the actions that are pursued by the SPCA or by yourself. You speak very authoritatively and you speak very positively in press releases about your course of action, and yet before this committee I must say that you have been lacking in a great deal of co-operation in helping us to decide what really you are after. In other words, what are your purposes?

I shot back, "In fairness, sir, I would have to state that the committee has give me little opportunity of being helpful to it. I have been subjected to vilification and abuse at a level that I just do not believe can happen in Canada: But I know it can because I have seen it."

MR. BORRIE: This is the part that also surprises me, Mr. Davies, that I cannot see where you say that you were vilified, because that is certainly not true of the committee. I can tell you that I do agree with you that you have had a very rough session. Some of the questions have been very direct and have been very forceful, but do not forget that over the years you have been very forceful in trying to stop an economy in the Gulf of St. Lawrence.

Gordon had the answer to that. "This was not a fact-finding mission. It was an anti-Brian Davies mission."

The Standing Committee on Fisheries and Forestry was not yet through with the seal hunt, and on May 20th, 1969, was at it again.

The main Government defence of the hunt has always been that the seals would destroy the Gulf fishing industry if the killing was stopped. In fact, evidence presented at this hearing refuted such nonsense.

In addition, the committee discovered that Brian Davies, although a "national nuisance" had helped the seals.

MR. WHELAN (*Committee Member*): Mr. Chairman, I would like to ask Dr. Sergeant a couple of questions. Are you a biologist, Dr. Sergeant?

DR. SERGEANT (*Biologist employed by the Canadian Department of Fisheries*): Yes.

MR. WHELAN: You have studied the life of the seal?

DR. SERGEANT: Yes, sir ...

THE CHAIRMAN (MR. GUY CROSSMAN): ... I was just wondering, Doctor, if hunting was discontinued in the Gulf, what would be the rate of increase in population over a three or four year period?

DR. SERGEANT: It would not increase we think by very much. In other words, since the Gulf population has not been overhunted it is not very much below its maximum which we suppose to be of the order perhaps of 1·75 million, assuming the present population to be about 1·25 million. We do not exactly know how this population is regulated except that the animals do not start to give birth until a later age. Even when we have low catches in particular years we can see this thing coming into effect, so that the thing would level off, but would not be very much higher than its present population.

MR. GOODE (*Committee Member*): Thank you Mr. Chairman. Mr. Dudka, how many assistants did you have to help discipline the seal hunt in 1964?

MR. DUDKA (*Department of Fisheries Field Supervisor*): I was not on the seal hunt in 1964, sir.

MR. GOODE: In 1965 then?

MR. DUDKA: In 1965, if I remember correctly, there were 21.

MR. GOODE: I see. Are there more people working in it

now or is it more mechanized now that you are inspecting the seal hunt better now than you were?

MR. DUDKA: Very much so. We go around to the different communities before the seal hunt and we bring them up to date on the regulations and we brief the hunters on what we expect. We are very well organized now and we are getting good co-operation from them.

MR. GOODE: Why are you better organized now than you were in 1965?

MR. DUDKA: We did not have the experience.

MR. GOODE: Why do you think you got the experience?

MR. DUDKA: Let me put it this way: Now I am more sure of what I am doing.

MR. GOODE: Would you say this resulted from whether this *Artek* film is a good one or whether it is misrepresenting the seal hunt, or was Mr. Davies a little more zealous in his pursuit than he should have been? Do you not think that these two things actually improved the discipline on the seal hunt?

MR. DUDKA: They might have some bearing on it and probably do. They keep us on our toes. Let us put it that way.

MR. GOODE: This is the point I was trying to make. Perhaps even though some of us on this Committee have been a little annoyed at some of the things that have been going on with the witnesses, nevertheless these two items, Mr. Brian Davies and the film, have considerably increased the discipline on the seal hunt?

MR. DUDKA: Yes.

Now to the seals eating all the fish.

MR. PERRAULT (*Committee Member*): I have one further question, Mr. Chairman, to Dr. Sergeant. If the seal fishery were abolished, what would be the possible effect on other fisheries?

DR. SERGEANT: I do not think there would be any easily observable effects. As a biologist, I look at it more the other way round, that if man continues to take more pelagic fish this may have an effect on the population of the seals ...

On Thursday, May 22, 1969, it was my turn, again. But it was a chastened committee that I faced.

Joanna Dupras, Ann Streeter, Barbara Malloch, Marjorie Bourke and Margaret Gurd, all good supporters of mine, had attended that first "Committee meeting". They had been infuriated with the proceedings. Together with Pat Shaw of Toronto, Mrs. H. Mackey of Ottawa, and Miss Copp of Vancouver they had organized a Canada-wide blitz of hostile mail to the Canadian Government. The volume of letters to the Prime Minister's office, for instance, was so great that form-type replies were sent out.

For its part, the press reacted violently to what many considered a dangerous infringement on civil liberties in Canada. The Committee had very badly burnt its fingers. Far from encouraging support for the seal hunt in Canada, it had done quite the reverse.

I faced, more or less, a rehash of the questions aimed at me at the last meeting, and really my appearing again was a waste of time and money.

At the end of the hearings the committee had interviewed a great many witnesses, beside myself. The film-makers for Artek Films, for instance, had come in for a severe grilling. But all that Parliament discovered was that some members of parliament were for the seal hunt and that opposed to the hunt was the vast majority of people in North America and Europe. I could have told them that at the beginning.

On October 15th, 1969, the Canadian Government released a statement on the seal hunt. The first paragraph read:

Canada will ban the hunting of "whitecoats" or baby seals in 1970.

CHAPTER SIXTEEN

Not Yet the End

F O R all practical purposes it is at this point in the story that the New Brunswick Society for the Prevention of Cruelty to Animals leaves the scene. For five long years the directors of the small Provincial SPCA had administered, very ably indeed, the "Save the Seals" Fund. But the bitter, bruising battles with government, the sealing industry and some sections of the press finally took their toll, and a small group comprising the most concerned directors incorporated a new organization—*The International Fund for Animal Welfare.* I was appointed Executive-Director and, without interruption, continued my work for the seals.

In retrospect, I believe the New Brunswick SPCA suffered through its association with a campaign that soon attracted the enmity of the *Telegraph-Journal,* the most influential newspaper in the Province. This newspaper held to an editorial policy which claimed that the drive [for the seals] employed unworthy tactics, blackened Canada's name abroad and sopped up donations that could be more usefully spent in the humane movement here and elsewhere. Personally, I could not accept their position and on one occasion met three senior staff members in an effort to explain our philosophy and tactics, but it did no good.

Actually, this newspaper strengthened my personality. As the editorials became more vitriolic and directed against me as an individual, I learnt to live with, and finally to ignore completely, what I considered to be *unreasonable*, hostile criticism, from any source. All that mattered to me was that I should conform to rigid ethical standards which I had set for myself and with singleminded determination get on with the job. Clearly, in New Brunswick I was going to win no popularity contest trying to save seals.

The same could not be said, however, for all the SPCA directors; and this is not meant as criticism. I believe a majority of them wanted to see the issue through to the end, but a smaller, influential group, considered the organization should concentrate on animal welfare in New Brunswick with some other body taking on the task of protecting seals. Amongst this second group were some who I feel were influenced by the *Telegraph-Journal* and others who thought I had been too boldly outspoken. In fairness to the conflicting needs of seals and of the animals in New Brunswick, the ways parted in 1969. Taking the assets, liabilities and with essentially the same objectives as the "Save the Seals" Fund, the International Fund for Animal Welfare set out to kill the dragon.

I have already written of the beauty of the Gulf of St. Lawrence harp seal nursery, and suggested that here was a tourist attraction of unparalleled loveliness. 1970 would be the year to test my theories. As far as I was concerned there was only one question: would the average person be so fearful at riding floating sea ice that he or she could not relax enough to enjoy the unique surroundings? Other problems involving weather, cost of transportation, etc., were mechanical and could be solved, if tourism surmounted this first hurdle, with money.

During the second week in March, and over a three day period, I took a total of twelve tourists to the seals. Flying out of the Magdalen Islands in two small helicopters this group, which included one lady with a damaged hip and walking with the aid of a cane, saw wild animals by

201

the thousand.

Enthralled humans photographed seals, touched them and watched in fascination as adult seals moved like quicksilver across the surface of blue water in open *leads*. The only sound of their passing was the wavelets lapping at a jagged and glittering ice floe. The majestic beauty and silence of nature's masterpiece was filled with life on a restless background of ice and sea. Later, more than one was to tell me their hours among the seals had been the most moving experience in their life. The first hurdle had been well cleared.

Granted that the seal herd is a wonderful sight and that ordinary people can move about the ice fearlessly, can tourism to the seal herd ever be an economically viable industry? I don't feel competent to judge but in any event, that is not the main consideration. For a few short weeks the ice and seals turn the Gulf of St. Lawrence into what could become a treasure-house of human experience. Tired, twitching humanity could step back a million years in time and come to the very root of nature. With eyes and heart overwhelmed by the magnificence of spectacle and ears throbbing with the deep silence, man would be home. What is profit compared to this? Canada owes the seals to Canadians, and Canadians owe the seals to the world.

All things considered, support for my point of view comes from an unlikely source. Speaking to the National Press Club in Canberra, Australia, on May 18th, 1970, Prime Minister Trudeau said, "Kids who blow their minds on drugs are missing a much better and cheaper thing—a trip into the Arctic or the Outback. It's habit forming, a habit that can't easily be kicked. It's wild! This was what 'turned on' several generations of Australians and Canadians long before the age of chemicals, and it can still turn us on if we don't let our urban hang-ups drive us to despair.

"To blow out pollution and monotony, I urge everyone to take such a trip if at all possible. It will help them find themselves. And it will help young Canadians and Australians to find again the spirit of their own countries.

"The great spaces of both countries, often thought of in terms of liabilities rather than assets, could prove to be 'our salvation'. They are not simply the over-burden of rich mineral deposits. They are our escape from the pressures of civilization—the balance wheel of our personal machinery. They must be husbanded and conserved."

It seems there is real hope. Prime Minister Trudeau is the one man with the power to create a sanctuary for harp seals—to make the splendor of the Gulf in Spring the "balance wheel" for so many. It now seems he also has the vision. How about it, Mr. Trudeau?

While I had been out with the tourists I had spent some considerable time photographing the seals. In particular, I had tried for shots of nursing animals. Crawling on my stomach I would work my way towards a mother and pup, hoping I looked like another seal, but it rarely worked. Even when I approached from up-wind most adult seals would recognize me as something other than one of them and would interrupt their nursing to keep a wary eye on me. Their vision seemed uncanny to me, especially for animals whose eyesight is supposed to be good only under water.

Occasionally I would come across a young mother who was obviously very proud of her new baby. I remember one in particular, greyish blue with dark spots and large wet eyes. Completely trusting, she allowed me to stroke her pup and, had I been daring enough, I am sure I could have touched her. I spent about an hour with this charmer, and during this time she viewed her baby from all angles with an occasional look of smug satisfaction directed towards me. Finally, she climbed onto a four foot high block of layered ice and resting on front flippers, for all the world like an indulgent human mother, looked down at her pup with an expression of the utmost tenderness. *The two seals were ten days away from the swinging clubs and blood soaked knives of the hunters.*

It was this year that I came across quite the loveliest animal it has ever been my luck to see. Another young female, but silvery grey in color with just a very few scattered dark spots. The set of her head and shoulders was such that she appeared to wear a draped hood. And what a hood! Silver in color, it formed a perfect frame for the beauty of her face, and her pose and obvious dignity brought to my mind pictures I had seen of the Madonna. *She was with her baby, and ten days away from the swinging clubs and blood stained knives of the hunters.*

Thoroughly soaked after hours of crawling around the ice on my stomach I still searched for the opportunity of a good shot of a nursing seal. Some little distance away I saw what appeared to be a nursing pair behind some jumbled blocks of ice. Hoping that my movement would be hidden by the obscuring ice, I crept forward. No sign of activity from the adult, but the white pup, later to be called Bingo, stirred restlessly and cried out. Cautiously, I crept forward to take what I hoped would be appealing photographs and then I felt something was amiss, the scene was not right. I stood up and walked quietly forward to find a pathetic tragedy.

The adult seal had apparently attempted to heave herself out of open water and onto the ice as the floes closed. In the split second necessary for her to reach safety the ice had moved with lightning speed to crush her. As yet unfrozen, she could not have been dead for long.

The lonely little orphan occasionally cried out and nuzzled his dead mother. Lying down beside her he cuddled closer to her cold body in a futile search for warmth and comfort. As I watched, the young seal urgently sought life from dead and empty breasts. When I left the ice that afternoon, Bingo rode the pontoon of my small helicopter.

Neill MacPherson, an employee of the Prince Edward Island Wildlife Park at North Rustico, P.E.I., volunteered to try to raise ten day old Bingo until he could be released, safe from hunters, at the close of the sealing season in late April. This arrangement, later confirmed by Charlie Bart- lett, owner of the Park, suited me fine. It did not involve the young seal in a long journey and, as the Park stood within sight of the Gulf ice, did not remove him too far from his natural environment. In addition, the Wildlife Park was famous for its handling of grey seals. Bingo now had the best chance I could give him.

Shortly after he arrived at the Park, Bingo created his first crisis. He resisted sucking from a bottle. I was in Europe at the time and the problem was turned over to that veteran seal handler, Joan Davies of Jack and Jill fame. Joan and Charlie Bartlett discussed the problem over the telephone and decided they would try the old Jack and Jill formula. Joan would fly to P.E.I. with the necessary ingredients and show Neill MacPherson how to intubate a sea mammal. The Park had never had such a young orphan seal before and had not faced the problem of a baby harp's refusal to suck from a bottle.

Nothing is easy, and immediately Joan had to find a substitute for whale oil. In desperation she turned to an ex- pert, Mr. Karl Karlsen of the seal hunt. Mr. Karlsen was helpfully courteous, and suggested she try calling Canada Packers in Montreal. Joan finally reached one of their scientists, a Mr. Glensost, who suggested she use herring oil and then saw to it that two gallons were Air Expressed to Fredericton. I could not help but think what a strange combination of people had combined their energies to save Bingo. And of course it demonstrated how unwise it is to think only in terms of absolutes. Mr. Karlsen, owner of many sealing ships could send his men to kill thousands of young seals, but he could also care about the life of just one.

After Joan had taken the Jack and Jill mixture to North Rustico and demonstrated to Neill MacPherson the tech-

SAVAGE LUXURY

nique of intubating seals, Bingo thrived. Neill has a way with animals and became very attached to our young seal. Bingo responded, and would follow his friend about the Park puffing and blowing as he hurriedly hauled himself along on his short front flippers. Bingo was being well cared for.

After all the beauty of the tourist project and the straining efforts for Bingo, the hunt, which opened on March 20th, was a shatteringly ugly experience.

Jack Davis had promised that no baby seals or whitecoats would be killed in 1970, and had suggested that most seals would be shot. This was hardly in the best interest of the seals concerned, but in the words of Prime Minister Pierre Trudeau, "Those who protest the killing won't be shown the same pictures of baby seals with their big blue or brown eyes."

On March 20th, I saw white baby seals brutally beaten by club swinging hunters, many of whom were finishing off their victims by kicking them. The same bloody, brutal business—the same high price of a sealskin coat.

On March 21st, I was with *Daily Mirror* reporter David Wright when a hunter started to skin what to me was an obviously live young seal. David later wrote, "I heard a 'dead' seal scream twice as the skinning knife was plunged into it—'a reflex action,' explained the hunter who, like most of his colleagues, was quite bewildered by the world interest in an occupation followed by his ancestors for 400 years."

What had happened to the promise that no baby seals or whitecoats would be killed in 1970?

The truth of the matter is that the Canadian Government intended no such relief for the young seals in the first place. Searching for a way to placate an aroused public opinion and still maintain the hunt, someone in that department of Government that deals with public relations, but little ethics, decided to call baby seals another name.

Picking on the seal hunter's expression for a baby seal that has shed its white coat "he" decided to call these infant animals, only 21 days old, "beaters" (blue/grey in color with dark spots). Then the world was glibly told that Canada would ban the killing of baby seals in 1970, or words to that effect. Buried in the "fine print" was the admission, little understood, that beaters would still be hunted. And the trick worked—I could sense a collective sigh of relief from the public.

Jack Davis intended to keep his promise that only beaters would be killed by delaying the start of the 1970 hunt until March 20th. By this time he could reasonably expect that virtually all of the baby seals would have finished their first moult. But nature was going to have none of that sort of trickery, and the ice formed late in the Gulf. The credibility of some people slipped badly as an audience of about 300,000,000 newspaper readers and television viewers saw, once again, white (as if the color mattered) baby seals beaten to death. The late ice had led to late pupping, and the young seals had not finished their moult.

The 1970 hunt was as bloody, brutal and sadistic as that of 1969. In spite of all the promises!

Other animal welfare societies observed the 1970 hunt and thickened the ranks of those opposed to the killing. Alice Herrington, dynamic President of the New York based *Friends of Animals* joined me on the ice and left promising, "I'll fight this monstrous slaughter to the end." *Beauty Without Cruelty,* a London based group, sent two observers to the hunt, Jean Le Fevre and Celia Hammond. Celia, a lovely English fashion model came away shocked, saying, "I don't think any woman could watch this and wear a sealskin coat again ... unless she was a monster."

The Fight For The Seals Must Go On. For my part, I believe my efforts have reduced the cruelty of the hunt, but that was not my primary goal. The question I pose for

207

the moral discrimination of Canada does not concern itself so much with how these animals are killed, but rather whether they should be killed at all. I see the seal issue as representing a showdown for wildlife. These animals are symbolic, and if they can't be saved it is probably not ever going to be possible to save any substantial population of wild creatures. The world will gradually fill with filth and one day, empty of all but man, this planet will become the loneliest place in the universe. *Perhaps in saving the seals, man may save himself.*

On April 19th Bingo was bursting with health and we were ready to release him. The hunters were gone, the fishing boat which was to carry him back to his sea home stood ready at hand. But the weather turned against us and we were forced to wait another day. April 20th dawned bright and clear and we prepared to set off, only to be stopped by the ringing of the telephone and bitter news. A rampaging male, a grey seal in the enclosure next to Bingo's had broken into the baby seal's pool and enraged by his presence had killed him. Here was the last tragedy of a tragic Spring.

Appendix A
REPORT TO THE NEW BRUNSWICK SPCA OF
OBSERVATIONS DURING THE 1968 GULF OF ST.
LAWRENCE SEAL HUNT

L. Karstad, DVM, Phd

I SPENT a total of 12 hours on the ice on March 18 and
19, 1968. These were the first two days of the seal hunt.
Part of the first hour was spent observing the killing and
skinning methods and photographing the operations. The
remainder of the time was spent examining skinned carcasses to determine the method by which they had been
killed and what lesions were produced. Most of the carcasses were examined after the sealers had left the areas.
This timing was intentional so that the presence of
observers on the ice would not influence the killing
methods. Some time was spent also examining live seals
and their reactions to stimuli.

Together with Dr. H. C. Loliger of Celle, Germany, I
examined 361 seal carcasses. Little time was spent on the
examination of carcasses with obviously crushed skulls. In
other cases, flesh was removed from the bones to search for
fractures and, in cases with no apparent fractures or where
only nasal bones were fractured, craniums were opened
and brains were examined for hemorrhages. Counting was

done with the aid of a mechanical hand counter. All observations were recorded immediately on tape and converted to written records each evening. Seals were examined in four different areas on the ice. Lesions were described in five categories:

(1) No grossly visible lesions, except those caused by the skinning operations.

(2) Cranium fractured without resultant hemorrhages.

(3) Cranium fractured with hemorrhages in the brain.

(4) Brain hemorrhages, with or without nasal bones fractured.

(5) Hemorrhages in the neck, ear, or nose areas, without grossly visible brain hemorrhages.

For convenience in tabulation, categories 1 and 2 were combined, since in both, evidence of prescribed killing methods were lacking. The data are summarized as follows:

Date	Area	I Cranium Fract. Brain Hem.	II Nasal Bones Fract. and/or Brain Hem.	III Hem. in Neck, Nose or Ear Areas	IV No lesions or PM Fract.
March 18	A	128	3	2	1
March 19	B	91	17	2	3
March 19	C	40	15	1	3
March 19	D	50	5	0	0
		309 (85.6%)	40 (11.1%)	5 (1.4%)	7 (1.9%)

The law states: "No one may strike a live seal except with the approved club and then only on its forehead." (Summary of Sealing Regulations, Department of Fisheries, Ottawa, February 15, 1968.) It was apparent that clubbings was the means and cause of death in all of the seals classified in categories 3 and 4; columns I and II in the table. These categories made up 96·7% of the total. The presence of brain hemorrhages in all of these animals is evidence that they were rendered unconscious by the blow or blows to the head. The nasal bones are contiguous with those of the cranium and together they compose the forehead portions of the skull.

Five or 1·4% of the seal carcasses examined had superficial hemorrhages in the neck, nose, or ear areas, without grossly visible brain hemorrhages. It is possible that the injuries in these cases were produced by clubbing but if so, the blow did not cause brain injuries severe enough to be visible to the unaided eye. It is possible, therefore, that some of these animals were not rendered unconscious by the blows.

A further 7 (1·9%) seal carcasses had either no visible lesions, except those produced by skinning, or they had skulls which appeared to have been fractured after death, probably after skinning. In such cases, the fractures were not associated with hemorrhages.

If, therefore, we combine categories 1, 2, and 5 (columns III and IV), we can say that 12, or 3·3% of the seals examined, did not have lesions which ensured that they would be unconscious when skinning was begun. They *may* have been unconscious; but we have no evidence from post-mortem examination that they were.

The sealing regulations (referred to above) state: "No one may hook, commence to skin, bleed, slash or make any incision with a knife or any implement until the seal is, without doubt, dead."

The exact time of death of an animal is difficult to determine, even by trained people. Witness the controversy over the legal aspects of hearts transplanted from humans who are pronounced "dead", yet from whose bodies living hearts can be obtained. The word "unconscious" may

211

therefore be more appropriate than the term "dead" in the regulation just quoted.

Even unconsciousness is difficult to ascertain in a young harp seal. Observations on the behaviour of whitecoat harp seals are that the animals have a normal response to human approach and/or handling which makes it difficult to determine in a quick, superficial examination, whether they are conscious, unconscious, alive, or dead. When disturbed, most normal whitecoat harp seals will retract their heads, close their eyes, stop breathing and lie without movement. Two or three minutes may pass before a seal in such a "trance" draws a breath. After it begins to breathe, it may remain without further movement for several minutes longer.

I did not subject a seal in such a "trance" to painful stimuli to see if it would react. It seems that this trance, or "freezing" reaction of harp seals is akin to that of the American opossum, *Didelphis virginiana*, which when "playing 'possum" can be subjected to otherwise painful surgical manipulations without giving any evidence of pain. A similar reaction can be elicited in other animals, including the hog-nosed snake (*Heterodon platyrhinos*). It has been said that these are fear reactions. Certainly they are natural reactions to dangerous situations. Opossum, hog-nosed snakes, and young harp seals cease to react in this way when they become accustomed to captivity and the presence of humans.

An important aspect of this "freezing" or "playing 'possum" reaction of harp seals is the difficulty it must present to the sealer to differentiate such a reaction from insensibility. Sealers were observed to club anywhere from three to a dozen or so whitecoats before returning to commence skinning. When sealers from different ships were working in the same area, several seals were clubbed and marked with a colored initial on the white coat, to establish their ownership until they could be skinned. In such

212

circumstance, it is possible that some seals might appear to be dead and might be skinned while in the above described "trance" reaction. I cannot say whether or not such an animal would feel pain. It may be unconscious.

I have drawn blood samples from opossums in similar "trance states" without observing the slightest reaction to the pricking and entering of the needle. Pain did not cause arousal.

Perhaps the question of whether or not the unresponsive baby harp seal is conscious or can feel pain could be answered by electro-encephalography. If this is to be attempted, it would have to be undertaken on the ice by an experienced person. I have not had experience with use of such equipment. The procedure would have to be done on the ice on unconditioned whitecoat subjects, because, as mentioned above, the animals would cease to react in this way when brought into captivity. Young harp seals in captivity were observed either to refuse to "play 'possum" when handled or they reacted only partially, withdrawing their heads and closing their eyes but still reacting to touching around their mouths and noses.

The point to be made is that present sealing methods may allow some seals to be skinned without being rendered certainly unconscious by clubbing. The sealer may not notice that an immobile seal has not been clubbed, when he begins the skinning operation. Such a seal may be in the described "freezing" reaction to the sealer's presence and may or may not be able to feel pain. Circumstances such as these may account for the observation that a small percentage of the seals did not have fractured skulls. If this explanation is correct, we have cases of unintentional contravention of the present regulations. Such errors might be prevented by making it unlawful for the sealer to club more than one seal at a time before beginning skinning operations. This would ensure, as well, that the occasional seal does not regain consciousness before the skinning operation is begun. Unconsciousness and insensibility, rather than death, should be the requirement, since the skinning operation is rapid and if commenced as soon as the seal is clubbed, the seal would have no opportunity to regain consciousness before the large axial blood vessels are severed, causing an abrupt drop in blood pressure and thus ensuring that consciousness will not be regained. (The axial, or brachial, blood vessels are routinely severed soon after skinning is begun, when the front flippers are separated from the body. The flippers remain on the skin or sculp, and are removed from the rest of the sculp later.) The sealer cannot readily determine that the seal is dead (unless of course he leaves it and returns much later). He can be certain, however, that a blow of the club which fractures the skull, will render the seal unconscious and that such an animal will die without pain during the skinning operation, if this is immediately carried out.

I did not see any instance of intentional contravention or disregard of the sealing regulations. A smaller percentage of seal carcasses (3.3%) were found without properly fractured skulls, as compared with percentages reported in previous seasons.